W9-AWN-017

Betterway Coaching Kids Series

COACHING YOUTH BASKETBALL

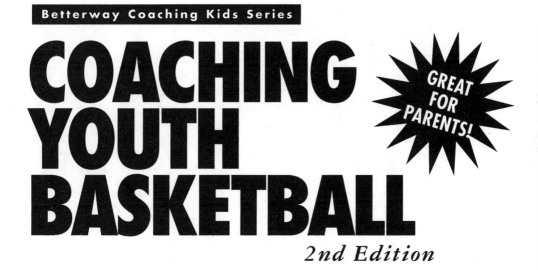

GREAT FOR PARENTS!

2nd Edition

John P. McCarthy, Jr.

BETTERWAY BOOKS
CINCINNATI, OHIO

To my grandson, John Connor McCarthy,
may there always be a dream in your heart.
With love.

Many thanks to the photo models: Hillsborough High Varsity Players
Megan Allen, Nicole Florentino, Joey and Jack McCarthy, Melissa Poch,
Steffanie Shoop. Also to Jaclyn Barton, Marshall Beveridge,
Jamie Capodiferro, Christopher and Scottie Demarest,
Lynn McCarthy, and Renee and Ryan Sigler.
Well done!

Coaching Youth Basketball. Copyright © 1996 by John P. McCarthy, Jr. Printed and bound in the United States of America. All rights reserved. No part of this book may be reproduced in any form or by any electronic or mechanical means including information storage and retrieval systems without permission in writing from the publisher, except by a reviewer, who may quote brief passages in a review. Published by Betterway Books, an imprint of F&W Publications, Inc., 4700 East Galbraith Road, Cincinnati, Ohio 45236. (800) 289-0963. Second edition. This book has been previously published as Youth Basketball: The Guide for Coaches and Parents.

Other fine Betterway Books are available from your local bookstore or direct from the publisher.

07   06   05   04   12   11   10

Library of Congress Cataloging-in-Publication Data

McCarthy, John P.
   Youth basketball: the guide for coaches and parents / by John P. McCarthy, Jr.—2nd ed.
      p.   cm.—(Betterway coaching kids series)
   Rev. ed. of: A parent's guide to coaching basketball. c1989.
   Includes index.
   ISBN 1-55870-414-0 (pbk. : alk. paper)
   1. Basketball for children—Coaching. I. McCarthy, John P., Parent's guide to coaching
basketball. II. Title. III. Series.
GV886.25.M37   1996
796.323'2—dc20   96-3022
                                                                                      CIP

Editor: Diana Martin
Production editor: Marilyn Daiker
Interior designers: Sandy Conopeotis Kent and Janet Finn
Cover designer: Sandy Conopeotis Kent
Cover photographer: D. Altman Fleischer
Interior photographs: John P. McCarthy, Jr.

TABLE OF CONTENTS

PREFACE

PREFACE

"Dad, I'd really like to get a lot of playing time next year, maybe even start in some varsity games." I could see how serious my son Jack was. He had played some basketball in grammar school, but had not made the freshman team in high school. As a sophomore, he was given a chance. He began to show his ability, and got good "playing time" on the J.V. team. Unfortunately, halfway through the season he slipped while re-bounding and broke his wrist.

He really wanted to contribute to his team the next year, but he knew he needed to improve a lot and make up somehow for lost experience. "OK," I said, "Let's go for it. I'll coach you this summer." I had played the game my whole life and knew I could help develop his skills. It worked out great! Jack made a major improvement and I had the best parenting and coaching experience of my life.

It was the summer of 1984. We worked nearly every day. At first, we concentrated on dribbling and practiced a lot of jump shots. We played a lot of one-on-one to refine his offensive and defensive skills. Our family took a four-week trip across country that summer. The rest of the family would groan as we spotted a basketball court on a prairie in South Dakota and pulled over for a quick forty-five minutes of practice. We practiced once in 110° Texas heat!

I would start under the basket and feed him rebounds for 10 to 15 foot jumpers until his arms nearly fell off. He would dribble with eyes closed, speed dribble 30 yard dashes, jump rope, pass against a wall at a close distance, and shoot fouls until he was exhausted.

That year no one could believe his improvement! He played a lot, and started some varsity games by the end of the season. This is a boy who was cut as a freshman! What's my point? A parent can make a difference!

I also coached my younger son in a clinic program for beginners. There I learned a lot about what kids need to do before they can be competitive. Remember, 85 percent of kids who play in grammar school or clinics will never play for their high school team. But, if they learn the game, they will play in lots and playgrounds for their whole lives. Get players just to hang in there until they learn the basics, and they will play this wonderful game for the rest of their lives.

You don't need to be a former (or current) basketball player to be a coach or the parent of an aspiring player. It helps, but it's not necessary. This book will teach you all you need to know. Even if you do not want to coach formally or are not athletically inclined, you can have a catch, feed rebounds, and be a companion to a child. This book will show you what to look for, how to spot errors in form. Most importantly, this book will focus on concepts, so you and young players can understand the *why* of things.

It's all here in this book. I have presented it in a way that a beginning coach or a parent who knows little about the game can nevertheless understand the concepts. Yet this book is not just for beginners, and the seasoned youth coach will get new insights into how to improve his or her approach. I focus on those things that can most quickly improve a player's chances of getting some quality playing time. The book also includes a full technical review of the game, and thus is useful in that respect for coaches and players at all youth levels. Good luck with it.

To Kids,

Jack McCarthy

Chapter One

THE GAME OF HOOPS

This book is written for coaches, parents and players at all levels of Youth Basketball, from beginning to advanced. No matter what your players' levels, it's *always* good to assume nothing and start with the basics. This chapter will begin to familiarize the reader with the jargon of basketball, and will also give a glimpse at the history of the game. Then we will cover the basic rules of play and will finish with a discussion of the various floor positions, including a review of the skills and abilities required for each position.

TEACH BASIC TERMS FIRST

Teaching basic terminology is a good way to start, and helps install confidence in your players. Knowledge of these terms will remove some of the mystery, the fear of the unknown. And it will help players get to the point where confidence replaces self-concern, where their perspective turns outward to the team and to the game instead of inward, worried about themselves, how they look, or whether they are doing OK.

I coached a clinic for eight-year-olds one year and was surprised to see how little the kids knew of the jargon, the language of basketball. They knew even less about the rules. Sure, they nearly all had heard of a slam dunk, but for many that was about it.

So before each practice, we sat around in a circle and I had a list of new words for them. Words like key, foul, walk, free throw, double dribble, three seconds, jumper, and lay-up. There are dozens and dozens of words like this that are unique to basketball. I'd do about ten words at each practice and we'd talk about their meanings. I'd first ask if any of the kids could explain the words to the team, to get a dialogue going. After this we would quickly review last practice's words.

It's important for players to be familiar with the basic terms. Sure, eventually they will get the *lingo*, but some kids get embarrassed when their ignorance is the basis for the day's lesson. You can avoid embarrassment by going over a few terms daily with your players, having them read this chapter on their own or going over this chapter with them. Be sure to read the Glossary at the end of this book. It will be an invaluable aid for teaching the jargon of basketball since it covers the most important terms and supplies ready definitions for your use.

THE HISTORY OF HOOPS

While the language of hoops is critical to coaching and learning the game, its history is nevertheless enriching. Surely, kids have been bouncing, kicking and throwing balls and round things for as long as there have been kids and round things. However, basketball seems to have a fairly definite point of invention.

Its Inventor

In 1891, a YMCA gym teacher in Springfield, Massachusetts, Dr. James Naismith, was trying to find something more interesting for his students to do during the winter months. So he nailed two peach baskets upon a balcony, which just happened to be 10 feet high, at either end of a gym floor. There were eighteen players in the class, nine on a side.

Dr. Naismith typed up a list of thirteen rules. The ball, a soccer ball, could be advanced by throwing or batting it with the hands. Players could not run with the ball but had to throw it from where they caught it. No physical contact was allowed. Dribbling was not introduced until some time later when a trapped player was allowed to throw the ball up and catch it. Floor dribbling came along even later.

Its Growth

The game was an immediate success. Women started playing almost right away, in 1892. During the early years, scores were low, usually well under ten goals per game. Colleges picked it up after the turn of the century. The sport grew most rapidly in the Midwest.

Standardization of Rules

Rules were standardized in the 1920s and 1930s. Free throws were no longer awarded for traveling violations, and the center jumps were no longer required after each goal. The game opened up. Fast breaks and other strategies made it quicker. The first national collegiate tournament, the National Invitational Tournament (NIT) was played in 1938 (Temple 60, Colorado 36) and the NCAA tournament followed in 1939 (Oregon 46, Ohio State 33).

Basketball Turns Professional

Professional basketball started early also, in New York and New Jersey, with local teams inviting teams from other towns. Leagues soon followed, developing from 1906 to 1920. Out of interleague competition came the National Basketball Association in 1949. That year Minneapolis, led by the great George Mikan, defeated Syracuse for the championship, six games to two. Over the years, great superstars have won the hearts of fans, Kareem Abdul-Jabbar, Wilt Chamberlain, Bob Cousy, Bill Russell, Elgin Baylor, Bob Pettit, Pete Maravich, Oscar Robertson, Rick Barry, Jerry Lucas, Magic Johnson, Michael Jordan, Larry Bird, Shaquille O'Neal. There are so many more of them, the all-time greats of basketball.

THE BASIC RULES TODAY

Modern basketball is a simple game. Popular games have to be simple since complex rules always spoil the fun of things. Your players can play better sooner by first learning the basic rules.

Two teams of five players each try to score goals by *shooting* a 29-inch round inflated ball through an 18-inch diameter cylindrical hoop which is 10 feet from the ground at the ends of a rectangular floor. They also endeavor to prevent the opponent from doing the same at the other end of the floor by *stealing* the ball or *blocking* a shot. The ball can be advanced only by *passing* to a teammate with the hands or by *dribbling* it on the floor. Play continues, unless the ball goes out of bounds, until a goal (two points) is scored. In either case the ball then goes to the opposite team.

Rules Violations

Play also stops upon a rules violation. A common violation is *walking*—taking steps without dribbling the ball. The penalty is to award possession to the opponent.

Another common violation is a *foul*—initiating illegal physical contact with an opponent. Fouls are usually committed by a defender, but may be committed by the offense, in which case they are called a *charge*. Upon a foul, the ball is awarded to the other team, unless the fouled player was shooting, in which case that player may shoot two *free throws*. When a team has accumulated six fouls in a half game, a free throw is thereafter awarded to the opposing team upon a non-shooting foul, and a second bonus shot is allowed if the shooter makes the first. This is known as *one and one*.

MORE RULES OF THE GAME

OK, let's dig a bit deeper! Here are some more rules which should be commonly understood. Be sure to check out the glossary for others.

1. A player may only dribble with one hand at a time. Kids, especially beginners, tend to bring the second hand in to help out, and that's a *double dribble* violation. Once a player ceases to dribble by grasping or touching the ball with both hands, she may not dribble again. (See Figure 1-1A.)

2. A closely guarded player can't hold or stationary-dribble the ball for more than 5 seconds or she loses it. (See Figure 1-1B.)

3. A player or team has ten seconds to advance the ball up court past the division (mid-court) line. Once the ball and both of the dribbling player's feet are past that line, the backcourt, that is, the half of the court behind him, becomes out-of-bounds for the offense for the remainder of that possession. Defenses often employ a *full court press*, meaning they attack the opponent in the backcourt area to slow them down. They are awarded the ball if 10 seconds elapse before the opponent crosses the mid-court line. Most beginner leagues prohibit the press since young dribblers have so much difficulty with it.

4. No part of an offensive player can remain within the offensive free throw lane—the 12-foot wide rectangle directly under the basket—for more than three seconds. The big players such as the *center* like to hang out directly under the basket, and the three-second rule prevents their hogging this valuable spot.

5. A player has only 5 seconds to inbound a ball, that is, pass it into play from out-of-bounds; and except after a goal, he must inbound from the spot designated by the referee. After a goal the ball may be inbounded from any point along that *end line* of the court. Aggressive defense here can give quite a payoff because the 5-second rule may pressure a player to inbound before a receiver is open.

6. Five players must start a game but as few as two can finish it. The latter situation is highly unusual, but could occur due to injury and/or ejection of players.

7. Illegal contact between opposing players are fouls. Many fouls occur when a defender tries to block a shot and hits the shooter's hand or bumps her with the body. Another common foul occurs when a defender reaches in to swat the ball and makes contact with the dribbler. (See Figure 1-1C.)

8. The 2-inch boundary lines around the court are out-of-bounds and neither the ball nor the foot may touch them when in possession of the ball. (See Figure 1-2.)

FIGURE 1-1

DOUBLE DRIBBLE, TIME OUT, REACHING IN

A. Double Dribble: A common mistake for closely guarded beginners is to use the free hand to help control the ball, which results in a double dribble violation. Players should keep their free hand away from the ball.

B. Time Out: When a player is closely guarded for more than five seconds, she either must pass, dribble or call a time out. To call a time out, a player should smother the ball, turn to the referee, make a T sign with the hands and yell "time out."

C. Reaching In: Reaching in is a common foul. Stress to your players that when they go for the ball, they must not make contact with the offensive player's body.

FIGURE 1-2
OUT OF BOUNDS

When dribbling, players should always be careful to not let their feet or the ball touch the sidelines and baselines, which are out-of-bounds.

9. A defensive player may not touch a shot ball in downward flight or *goaltending* will be called and the points are awarded as if the shot had been made.

10. Players may not try to disconcert a free thrower. Once the free thrower has the ball no one may enter or leave a marked lane space. Players may not enter the free throw lane to rebound until the ball leaves the shooter's hand. The shooter may not enter the lane until the ball hits the rim or backboard.

11. According to the Principle of Verticalization, although a defensive player does have a right to the space directly over him and may jump straight up without fouling, most referees will nevertheless call a foul on the defender if contact with an opposing player is made. The best advice to give your players is, when on defense, hold their ground, raise their hands, and stay still.

How to Get More Information

This is only a thumbnail sketch of the game's main points. It's enough to get going. There are other frequently used rules which I'll cover later in this book, and some minor ones, which are described in the glossary along with the jargon of the game. You can order a book outlining the official rules from the National Federation of State High School Associations

(11724 Plaza Circle, Box 20626, Kansas City, MO 64195, (816) 464-5400) for a cost of $5.00 plus $4.00 shipping.

THE COURT AND EQUIPMENT

Basketball court sizes will vary depending on the age of your players. The gyms in many middle schools are about half the size of the usual 50' × 84' high school gym. The gyms in most schools at the seventh or eighth grade levels are the larger size. (See Figure 1-3A.)

The *backboard* is a rectangular or semicircular fan-shaped surface on which the basket is mounted. It is also referred to as a *bangboard* or *bankboard* because of its use for bank shots, or it is called the *glass*, if so constructed. In outside lots, it's usually made of wood or metal. (See Figure 1-3B.)

The basketball itself is usually leather. The circumference must be 29½ to 30" for boys and an inch less for girls. Weight is 20 to 22 ounces for boys, 2 ounces less for girls. It should be inflated to a pressure so that it will bounce to a height of 49 to 54" at the top when dropped from more than 6' high.

PLAYING OPPORTUNITIES

No more than five players from each team are on the floor at any one time, with youth teams usually numbering between twelve to eighteen players. This means a lot of kids either won't make the team or won't get much playing time. Fortunately, below sixth or seventh grade, and sometimes all the way up to high school age, many towns run clinic or in-town recreation programs that let anyone who wants to play do so. Some of these clinics limit team size and require equal time or at least a certain minimum time for all players. I like this for a number of reasons. With determination, dedication and practice, even kids who get height and/or coordination much later than others can, over the years, win out over more natural athletes. Very often the kids who start varsity in high school were not the best players at the grammar school level. Without the "equal opportunity" offered by public clinics, many young players would never realize their potential.

ABOUT HEIGHT, SPEED, AGILITY AND MORE

The old adage is that basketball is a big man's game. This is an overstatement, and is certainly not always the case at the youth level. However, there is no question that height helps a lot when defending or shooting underneath the hoop, and the highest percentage shots *are* close to the

FIGURE 1-3A

THE BASKETBALL COURT

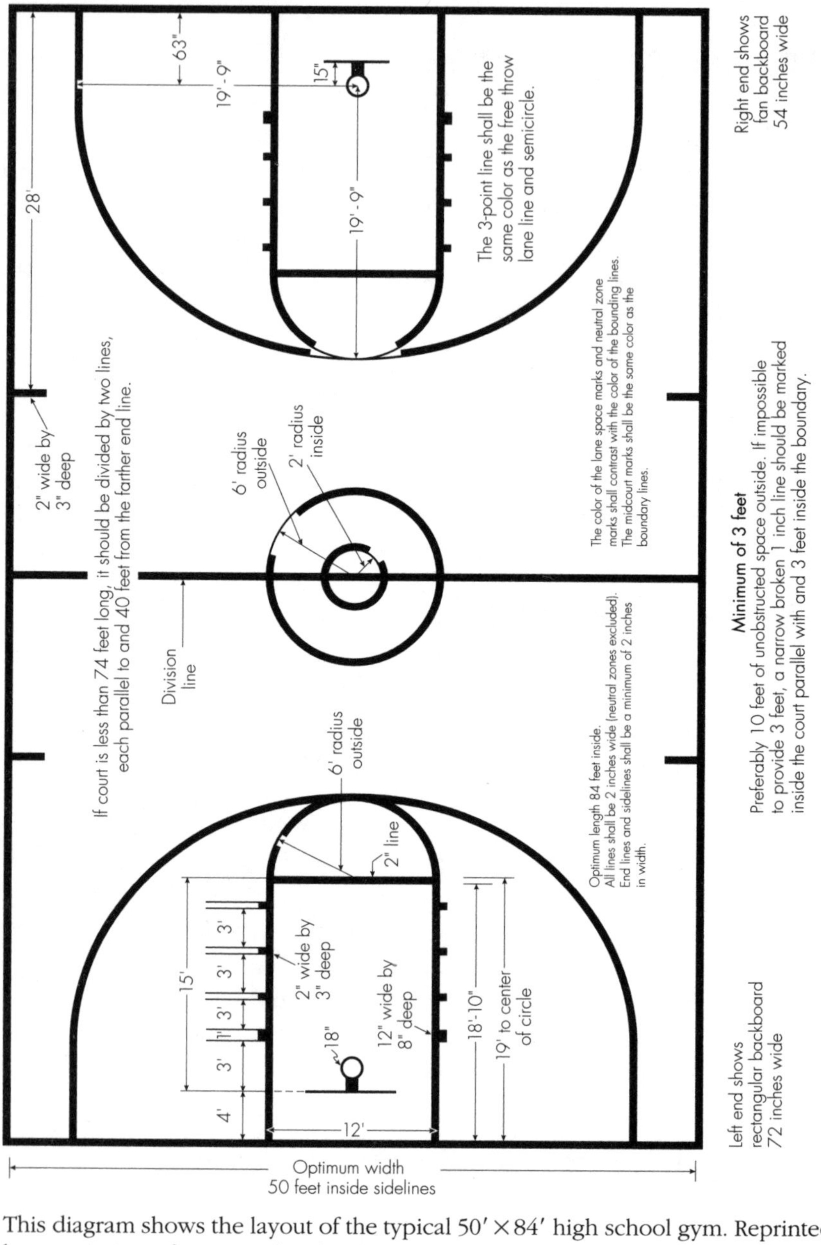

This diagram shows the layout of the typical 50′ × 84′ high school gym. Reprinted by permission of State High School Association.

FIGURE 1-3B

THE BACKBOARD

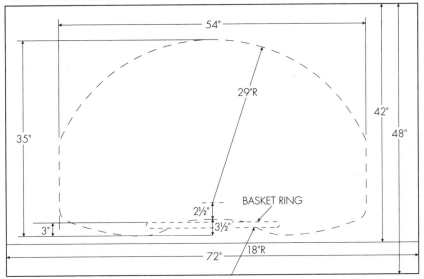

According to National Federation rules, the backboard construction may be glass, wood or metal, and can be a rectangle 6′ × 4′ or 6′ × 3.5′, or a 54-inch fan shape, as shown above.

basket! But, when you get down to it, that's about all you need height for. Rebounding has more to do with positioning than with height. Also, at the young ages, the height differential is usually much less than it is for adults. The point I'm making is that you should not discourage a child from playing basketball if she is not tall. It's a game she can enjoy for her entire life, so urge her to learn it.

So while height is a very important element, speed, agility, leadership, a good outside shot, good dribbling, good passing, aggressiveness and quickness are also needed and can compensate for short stature. Often, the tall youths have only their height and are otherwise less coordinated since they grow so fast. Believe me, I know. I was one of them.

I must repeat, basketball is a game your children or players can enjoy their entire lives. I've played it all of my life, and still do. It's a great game, good exercise and a super way to meet people. Encourage players to hang in there and play for a few seasons. Even if a kid is not playing much, he is practicing and learning the game. This experience alone will let a child join in playground pickup games for the rest of his life.

BASKETBALL POSITIONS

Generally in basketball the taller players play underneath the hoop or along the baseline, at the *center* or *forward* positions, and shorter players fill the *guard* positions, where speed is more important. There are usually one center, two forwards and two guards on the floor. Forwards are sometimes called *power forwards* or *shooting forwards* depending on whether they are generally called upon, in the plays selected by the coach, to play close to the hoop (the former) or to shoot from the outside (the latter).

Guards also are categorized. One is called a *point guard*, known more for ball-handling and play-making. Point guards get their name because they dribble the ball up court to the *point*, the spot on the circle surrounding the free throw line farthest from the basket. It is from here that they initiate offensive plays. The second guard is usually called an *off guard*, because he is located *off* the point in the wing area depicted in Figure 1-5. The *off guard* is usually the team's best outside shooter and often shoots from his wing position. He is also is called upon to be an *outlet* guard, that is, the person to whom a player underneath passes the ball after a rebound. Nowadays, more teams tend to get away from traditional designations, using numbers or floor positions to designate players. The use of numbers or floor positions is covered in chapter five when we discuss play making. For now, let's discuss each position.

The Center

The tallest kid on your team will usually play at the center position. Her court area is mainly in *the paint*, the area under the hoop between the free throw lines.

Center On Offense

The main job of the center on offense is to get open for the pass underneath, that is, in the paint, and take the high percentage *lay-up* or *hook shot*. He *must* be able to catch quick passes! A center also looks to *pick off* defenders by using his body to block a defender's path, freeing a teammate to drive for a shot. Finally, a center looks for rebounds, particularly offensive rebounds, and tries to score with them.

Post Positions—The majority of a center's actions occur at a *post position*. The post positions are found along the foul line. Up by the free throw line, it is called a high post. Close to the basket it is called a low post. Remember when posting that the foot cannot be inside the three-second area for more than three seconds without your center receiving a violation.

FIGURE 1-5

FLOOR POSITIONS

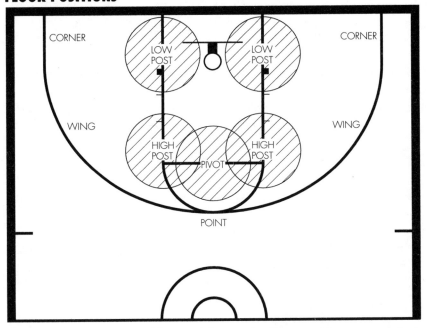

Floor position names vary a bit around the country. Some coaches even use numbers, rather than terms. The main floor positions are the corners, wings, low and high posts, and the pivot.

These violations drive coaches crazy. It's OK to slide in and out of a post position to avoid the violation. (See Figure 1-5.)

Shots—A low-post position sets up a center's shots. A high post position is used more for play-making, picks, give and go's, and many other plays discussed more fully in chapter five.

Centers must know how to shoot hook shots, and should learn to shoot left-handed underneath. These shots are covered in chapter four. If your player is tall, make him practice underneath the hoop, in the paint. Sure, he should practice outside shots: They are part of the game and he will need them to be a fully rounded player. But, unless he has a great outside shot, his team will need him underneath, where you as coach must tell him to stay.

Emphasize short jump shots, lay-ups, hook shots, chippies, using both hands, fakes, fake pumps, tap-ins, pivot steps, all with minimal dribbling—these are skills he will need to perfect.

Posting Up—On offense, your center's most effective weapon is the *post-up*. In this position, the center stands with her back to the hoop and the defender. She stretches her arms out for a pass, leaning slightly into the defender. Underneath the hoop, players without the ball are usually allowed to make light contact, jockeying for position, but cannot push, shove or bump each other. This effectively screens the defender from stealing a pass, and allows the center to *put a move on* the defender, that is, a quick maneuver to get a shot off. Posting-up is particularly effective when the center is taller than the defender.

The steps are:

1. The center heads to the low post, the area by the large block next to the foul line under the hoop area.

2. Through his positioning, he feels the defender on his posterior, and keeps him in between his elbows, using the elbows and hands to feel the defender, even to control him a bit.

3. The center, or post player, must make himself feel wide, and work his way backward without fouling. If the defender is directly behind the center, the center fakes a move in a side direction in order to move the defender to one side.

4. Once the defender is to one side, the center moves hard to the other side, pivots around the defender as if he were a post, holds the ball (or dribbles no more than once) and then explodes upward. He shouldn't throw the elbow, but should keep it out for protection and to pick up a possible foul. Employ body fakes and shot fakes as needed.

The Head and Shoulder Fake From Post Position—The *post play* is a maneuver around the post position, however, as suggested above, it is made easier if fakes are added to the movement. Perhaps the best move out of a low post is to head and shoulder fake to one side, and then to *drop step* quickly the other way. A drop step is simply a step back with the inside foot (toward the hoop!) and a spin for the shot. This move anticipates that the defender will initially go with the first fake. It is essentially a pivot or post backward and a shot off the dropped foot. Of course, if the defender is already to one side, then no fake is needed and the player just drop steps with the other foot. The drop step can be used on either side of the lane, and can be used for an inside or an outside pivot. (See Figure 1-4.)

Practicing Moves—Given all of the above, it makes sense for your center to focus on and regularly practice all the moves which can be made from the post position.

FIGURE 1-4
POSTING UP

Step 1. To *post up*—an effective way to set up a pass reception and a shot—keep the defender "in the elbows" and back up as the ball is about to be passed.

Step 2. Fake to one side, keeping the feet stationary.

Step 3. Drop step to the right foot, then quickly spin clockwise.

Step 4. Turn, take a hook shot. Posting up can be done on either side of the lane.

The most common post move is usually to fake right and move left (from a post on the right side of the lane) for a lay-up, a hook shot or a fading short jump shot. (See chapter two on Shooting.) To be able to set up the move, the center needs to practice the footwork required to fake right/go left, or fake left/go right. Remember, big players use power from the post position and smaller players must rely more on speed, positioning and fakes. Practice accordingly.

It's helpful for a coach or parent to play a budding center one-on-one from the post position. It's great experience for everyone. Watch the walks!

Avoid Dribbling Out of a Low Post Position—A common bad habit of centers is the natural tendency to put the ball down or dribble it underneath. The pivot step is usually enough to cover whatever distance is needed out of a low post. Sure, there are times a single dribble is needed to punctuate a fake, or to get closer to the hoop, but more often than not, the need for the dribble is just a failure to use the pivot step properly. Dribbling underneath is an invitation to have the ball stolen or bobbled in what is usually very heavy traffic.

Center On Defense

On defense, your center must dominate the paint area and keep the opponents from shooting the high percentage underneath shots. This involves *fronting*—getting the body or a hand in front of an opponent trying to post-up underneath—in order to prevent the pass underneath. It also involves blocking shots and otherwise harassing anyone driving into the paint area.

Centers usually pick up a lot of fouls playing defense, particularly at young ages. This is because there is a lot of action and traffic underneath and also because of inexperience. Blocking shots takes height or leaping ability, because the ball should be blocked far enough from the shooter to avoid a foul. Also, the preferred technique is to block across the ball, not toward the shooter, to minimize the chance for a foul. Whenever two kids go up very close to each other, chances are there will be some body contact. If your center is moving, or is off the ground and any body contact is made, a foul will be called. So a center must know that unless she can dominate the shooter, the best technique underneath is just to stand still with arms raised straight up, trying to put some pressure on the shot or even draw an offensive foul. If the defender is still and contact is made, it's an offensive foul or charge. The best defense against a player driving for a lay-up is to establish position in front of that player, stay still and take the offensive charge.

FIGURE 1-6
BOXING OUT

Boxing out an offensive player is an effective way to get rebounds. These two defenders demonstrate great box-out positions because their bodies are low and wide.

Rebounding—Perhaps the most important defensive responsibility of the center is to get *rebounds*. If the other team gets the rebound, it's an easy shot and two points. Therefore, it's essential when defending to get rebounds. This shouldn't be difficult, since defenders are usually positioned between their opponents and the hoop, and should already be better positioned for the rebound.

Boxing Out an Opponent—A key defensive strategy is to *box out* the opponent as a shot is taken. For the center this is critical. Upon release of a shot by an opponent, the center hesitates a second before turning to face the hoop for the rebound. This hesitation allows the center to see in which direction the opponent is going to get to the rebound. Then your center should step in the opponent's way, rotate her back after the opponent is blocked off, stick her posterior into the opponent and outstretch her arms sideways a bit to make it tough for the opposing player to get around, thereby *making herself wide*. (See Figure 1-6.) Once the center gets the rebound, she looks to the sideline for a teammate, usually a guard, designated as the *outlet*, and passes to her. We'll discuss this more in chapter five.

The Forward

Forwards are taller players, usually the next tallest after the center. They need to be tall because, like the center, they are frequently called upon to play underneath the hoop; however, forwards also cover the wing area and the corners of the court, so they need to develop an outside shot, preferably near the baseline, and they must be able to dribble and pass.

Every position on the team requires some skills unique to that position: For forwards, it's the corner shot and the baseline drive, described in this chapter. Of course, forwards need to be complete players and need to develop all skills of the game, but you should emphasize and practice the skills most often required of them. This is where the parent can be most helpful, assisting in the practice of those special skills. Forwards spend a lot of time in the corner or baseline area, and they need to perfect their skills from that location and perspective.

Forward On Offense

On offense, the first duty of the forward, besides following the steps required of offensive pattern plays covered in chapter five, is to get free for a pass. Most teams will have a series of plays, or a normal offensive routine, requiring the forward to catch a pass from the guard, move sharply through the free throw lane or make some moves underneath. However, many offensive routines start with a pass to the forward in the corner.

Key Move for the Forward—Your forward needs to develop a move which frees him up for a pass. The best move is to fake a run to the center, taking a few quick steps toward the center, and then quickly dart back to the corner for the pass. The idea for any fake is to relate to the defender. Once the defender commits to following the fake, your forward darts back the other way. (See Figure 1-7.)

Handling the Ball—When the forward gets the ball, she simply follows the offensive routine. Usually someone moves to the hoop for a possible pass or the center posts-up low for a pass. Someone may come out to *pick* the defender guarding your forward, freeing her up to drive to the hoop. Otherwise, the forward may need to make her own way, fake outside and drive the baseline, or jab step and take a jump shot. If all else fails, she should pass the ball back out to a guard and start another offensive series.

Because forwards often get the ball in the corner, too far away to shoot, they need to be able to pass the ball effectively. The two-hand overhead pass to low post is one such pass. Others are described in chapter four.

Forwards are sometimes called upon to play under the hoop, so all

FIGURE 1-7
CORNER JAB

Step 1. The *corner jab step* opens up a corner player for a pass. First, take some sharp steps inside to get the defender in motion.

Step 2. Then dart suddenly back to the corner for the pass.

offensive and defensive skills mentioned for centers—posting, hook shots, boxing out, fronting a player, avoiding fouls, taking charges and rebounding—must be practiced.

The Baseline Drive—Unique to the forward position on defense is preventing the *baseline drive*. (See Figure 1-8.) Forwards *never* want an opponent to successfully drive inside, that is, between them and the baseline. If that occurs, the likelihood of a score increases dramatically for the opponents. Forwards should always close off the baseline drive with the leg closest to the baseline. Their teammates can help in the other direction.

Fake Shot and Drive—The forward also needs to defend against the *fake shot and drive*. Because there is a strong natural tendency to try to block outside shots, the fake shot and drive move is usually very successful even at younger ages. We'll discuss this all in more detail when we discuss defense in chapter six. We'll also talk about how to defend the outside shot.

FIGURE 1-8
BASELINE DRIVE

Preventing an offensive baseline drive is a responsibility unique to your defensive forwards. Here, the defender failed to get her hip and leg out far enough to protect the baseline, which allowed the corner forward to drive the line.

The Guard

It's said basketball is a big person's game, and height certainly is a key attribute. Nevertheless, there is plenty of room for shorter players.

Guards are usually the shortest players on the team. However, keep in mind that in the pros, the guards are often about 6 feet, 4 inches tall. It's all relative. The biggest guys (the seven footers!) are usually needed underneath. In 1988, I enjoyed watching Trenton State College games. A friend's son played on the team, which had a good shot at the Division III National Championship. The team also had a 5 foot, 7 inch guard named Greg Grant who eventually broke the all-time national scoring record for collegiate careers with over 2,600 points, and went on to play pro ball. Greg was the ultimate guard, and a wonder to behold.

Dribbling

A guard needs to be able to dribble effectively with either hand. He needs to be able to take a defender one-on-one and dribble around him. He needs to be able to dribble in close quarters and heavy traffic, and to speed dribble at a dead run. The kid on the team who can dribble the best should bring the ball up the floor. If a team doesn't have a guard who can get the ball down the court, it will fail miserably. For players at young ages, local rules often require the defense to wait until the ball crosses mid-court before attacking the ball, as noted earlier. This is a welcome rule.

You must emphasize it in team and in personal practice. Your guards can practice anywhere, because they don't need a basketball court to dribble. Since dribbling is the most effective skill in basketball, your players should practice dribbling one-on-one. A guard should dribble while another player tries to steal the ball. It's the best possible practice.

Passing

Next in importance to dribbling, guards need to be able to pass the ball deceptively, accurately, and with strength and speed on the ball. (See chapter four.) In general, your guards should know where their teammates are, dribble with their heads up and eyes scanning the play, and spot the open teammate. The kid who does these best should be your point guard.

The Point Guard

The point guard is your quarterback. He positions himself at the top of the key—the point of the free throw circle farthest from the basket—and starts the offensive play. A point guard needs to be able to shoot outside and drive inside. Although these skills are not as important as dribbling and passing, shooting ability always helps. Usually, if your team has one good outside shooter, that's all you really need. If a player shows promise with the outside shot, practice it with him.

The Shooting Guard

A shooting guard is called an off guard and usually plays the wing area, between the guard and the forward areas. She may have a favorite spot where she shoots the best and where she will hang out.

Guards On Defense

Defensive guards need to steal passes. A kid who can steal passes is very valuable because a stolen pass usually leads to an easy score. Chapter six deals with this skill in more detail. Defensive guards pressure the outside shooter and, more importantly, ensure that the ball carrier doesn't drive by them. Stress to your guards that the key to good defense is preventing penetration and keeping the opponent away from the high percentage shots.

Chapter Two

SHOOTING

Shooting is fun. It's the essence of basketball. I'll never forget the smiles that broke across the faces of kids as they made their first basket ever in a game. It was a rite of passage.

A kid who can consistently hit shots, especially jump shots, is a rare and valuable player. Teams often build their offense around their best shooter by running plays that get this player free for a good shot. Kids know who can shoot the ball. Coaches know too. If a kid can shoot, he's told to go for it. If a kid can't consistently make a certain shot, he's told not to waste the shot. It has nothing to do with personalities, at least it shouldn't. If your players have it, use it, otherwise they should only do what they can do. It makes sense.

It is not essential to be a good shooter, but if a kid can't shoot, he will need to be very good at dribbling and passing or rebounding. Role players such as these are important too! Most kids will not become great shooters, and so it's important to develop other skills.

TYPES OF SHOOTERS

There are outside shooters and inside shooters. A good outside shooter is someone who can sink at least half her shots from 12 feet or farther. They are the chosen people of basketball. A winning team almost always has a good outside shooter. I played in a youth league as a kid and we had a great shooter named Rich. He scored twenty points a game and led us to a championship. It was great to know he was on the court and would stick the ball when things got close!

Everyone on the team must be a decent inside shooter. Tall players will obviously be called upon to do most of it, but everyone needs to be able to deliver two points most of the time when shooting underneath. An inside shot takes a sense of touch because it is banked off the backboard or soft-touched gently over the rim. A player must know how hard and where to hit the ball against the backboard. Young kids usually bank it too hard and the ball bounces away off the rim.

Shooting Can Be Learned

The good news is that shooting can be learned. Sure, naturally talented kids will learn a lot faster and shoot with a higher percentage, but *all* kids can learn to shoot. It takes thousands of shots to significantly raise a shooter's percentage, but remember, it really doesn't take that long to shoot a thousand shots!

Good Coaching Is Key

The best way to teach shooting is simply to help a kid shoot that thousand shots. In 1984, I had an experience with my older son, Jack, which was the most memorable coaching experience of my life. I mentioned it in the preface but it bears repeating here. I think it's a great testimony to what an individual parent can do, and it may be the best story I can leave you with in this book.

Jack was entering his junior year in high school. He had played basketball, but for a number of reasons, including injuries, he had not gotten a lot of playing time or experience.

Jack was tall and quick, and very much wanted to be able to contribute more during his final two high school years. He and I discussed it, and we agreed that we would spend the summer in an intensive program.

We spent hours every day during the summer working on skills. I would stand under the hoop and rapidly feed him rebounds for short jump shots. He shot and shot until his arms nearly fell off. He would dribble, shoot fouls and play one-on-one against me. By the time we were done, he *couldn't miss* short jump shots. His school coach told me he had never seen such improvement, and Jack eventually broke into the starting lineup. This is a boy who was cut as a freshman!

The experience taught me how much difference a parent can make in helping a child improve, especially when the child is motivated.

You need to be patient with young kids because they develop shots at different paces. I coached a clinic for eight- and nine-year-olds a few years ago. A boy named Eric was one of the most talented athletes in the group, but he was so full of energy that he couldn't make a basket. He just banged the ball off the backboard. When Eric was twelve, I saw him play on my son's school team. He was still rough, but you could see the beginnings of gracefulness. The boy will be a great player someday; for him, and for many kids, it just takes time and perseverance.

Perhaps the greatest contribution a coach or parent can make is to help a player get beyond the frustrating experience of being a beginner. Help him or her hang in there!

ABOUT OUTSIDE SHOOTING

The introduction of the three-point play, a long shot of over 19 feet, has restored outside shooting to basketball at the high school and college levels. At youth levels, most kids can't shoot that far. However, it brings a needed dimension back to the game, and gives shorter players a chance to develop a skill which will give them more playing time.

In practice, give your kids a chance to show what they have. And stress to them that an outside shot, in particular, is not developed during team practice. A player must do that on his own time. It takes ten thousand shots. My younger son played with a boy named Matt, who spent hours nearly every day, even in the rain, shooting jump shots in his driveway. Because of this practice, the boy can shoot, and he will always be allowed to take the outside shot. It's a privilege which must be earned. This is not to say that other players can't shoot from the outside from time to time, but it is in your team's best interest for kids to do what they do well, and most of the time that's all they should do. They should shoot from a distance at which they can make a shot at least half the time.

We'll cover offensive play-making in chapter five. Suffice it to say that a play is a series of movements designed to free up a shooter, usually by screening or picking off the player who is defending him. If the play works, a shooter is open to take a high percentage shot. High percentage shots are mainly shots within the player's range, which are taken with a minimum of defensive pressure, thus allowing the shooter to use good shooting form.

The Mechanics of Outside Shooting

We've already covered some of the advantages of outside shooting. Now, let's discuss the mechanics.

The Triple-Threat Stance

The triple-threat stance is a multipurpose position from which the player can shoot, dribble or pass in any direction, and fake. The weight is forward on the balls of the feet. The feet are balanced under the shoulders and pointed toward the basket. The knees and waist are bent, ready to move in any direction; head and shoulders are square and level; head and chin are up; the ball is up in front of the chest; elbows are out to protect it. (See Figure 2-1.) We'll cover the triple-threat stance again in the chapters on offensive and defensive dynamics.

Fake Moves Open Up Shots

A fake move is used by a closely defended shooter to throw the defender off balance and open up an unobstructed shot. Usually, a faked dribble

FIGURE 2-1

TRIPLE-THREAT STANCE

The *triple-threat stance* requires that the player's weight is forward on the balls of the feet, knees and waist are bent, head is up, shoulders are square and the ball is held up by the chest.

or jab step will get a young defender to move to the side or to back up a bit. As soon as the shooter gets the ball, she jab steps strongly and directly toward the defender. When the defender reacts and takes a step back, the shooter takes the shot.

Another great fake move is to raise the ball high very quickly as if to shoot. This causes the defender to come forward and allows the ball handler to dribble past him. A combination of jab steps and fake shots often creates a good scoring opportunity and should be automatic whenever a player, especially a guard, gets the ball. (See Figure 2-2.)

You can't overemphasize to your players the importance of fakes. If a defensive player gets a hand up in your shooter's face, the shooting percentage drops considerably. Communicate this concept by telling the child to try to *feel* the defender's balance. The player tries to mentally push the defender off balance into one direction or the other and can almost feel when the defender leans one way or the other. Trying to relate to the defender's balance helps make the fake more convincing. The defender

FIGURE 2-2
JAB STEP AND SHOOT

Step 1. The *jab step* is a good way to cause a defender to move to the side or to back up. First, jab step right at the defender.

Step 2. When the defender backs off, snap back and shoot.

must believe that the shooter is going to dribble. Practice this by having your players work in pairs, faking each other.

Jump High and Straight Up

The highest percentage jump shot is straight up. A straight jump gets the ball higher and over the tips of the defender's fingers, which reduces the odds that the shot will be blocked.

Players sometimes lean to one side as they jump, which results in a slight ball motion to that direction. Sure, defensive pressure forces a shooter to lean, or fade away (lean backward), and sometimes (not often) a player can even perfect such a shot. But the higher percentage is always straight up, thus ensuring that the shooter does not have to calculate and compensate for body lean. (See Figure 2-3.) Teach your players to jump as high and as gracefully as possible, involve both feet, and spring off the toes. Players should practice feeling the balance in their feet before jumping. The ball is released just before the peak of the jump, which gets the force of the legs into the shot. Stress to your team that shooting starts in the legs. Talk about the lazy jump shot, an overly relaxed shot without significant height in the jump. Such a shot can be more easily blocked, and is less accurate and intense. Using both feet adds to the balance and control of the jump, thus improving the odds for a goal.

FIGURE 2-3
JUMP STRAIGHT UP

The highest percentage shots, that is, those that are successful most often, are made with the body straight, not leaning toward the hoop.

Executing the Shot

For an outside shot, the hands form a cradle for the ball which is held high, in front of and over the head to minimize the chances of a blocked shot. This allows the player to see the basket from underneath the ball, between the arms. Begin with the shooting hand behind and a bit lower than the ball, the arm close to the body and bent at the elbow. The non-shooting hand should be straight up on the opposite side so that the player is in control of the ball but not squeezing it. His hands should be soft, handling the ball like a fragile egg on a launching pad. The head and shoulders are level and square so that the body is balanced and erect. (See Figure 2-5.)

FIGURE 2-4

CRADLE HIGH, SHOULDERS SQUARE AND POINT ELBOW

Shooting with the elbow angled outward, as shown by this player, is the most common flaw for beginners.

Here the arm is kept parallel with the body, the elbow pointing toward the hoop. The hand cradles the ball slightly above the head, and the shoulders are square.

The most important aspect of outside shooting is the position of the shooting elbow, *which must aim toward the basket.* Often kids point that elbow outward a bit. *Keep the elbow in.* More than anything else, even more than a body lean, an outward elbow will send a ball in an errant direction and will prevent the wrist from properly launching the ball. The upper shooting arm should be, generally, parallel to the floor, and it must always point in the direction of the basket. (See Figure 2-4.)

At the top of the jump, flick the wrist, placing a 30° spin on the ball with the thumb side of the hand. Only one hand shoots, the other is passive and simply falls away. (Kids often shoot with two hands, since they are not strong enough to shoot with one. However, they must understand that one-handed shots are higher percentage shots.) Shoot just at or before the top of the jump, again to avoid the defender's outstretched hands and to ensure that some of the strength of the jump is transferred to the ball. A shot begins in the legs and the power is transferred to the ball.

The Gooseneck Wrist Flick

The *gooseneck wrist flick* is as important to shooting as pointing the elbow at the hoop is. Most kids develop all kinds of crazy hand techniques, such

FIGURE 2-5

CRADLE THE BALL HIGH

In preparation for shooting, the hands cradle the ball slightly above the head, with the shooting hand beneath the ball and the guiding hand to one side.

as closing the fingers into a fist as they shoot, or coming down with the middle finger or the pinkie finger. The natural and correct form is to flick the ball out of the cradle by turning the palm down and out. The little finger stays in the same position, pointing upward, before and after the shot. The thumb and index finger however move forward, down and out. The index finger does most of the work of shooting.

When the shooting hand turns down and out, this puts a reverse 30° (from the vertical) spin on the ball. That's how you know it has been done properly. (See Figure 2-6.) The final position of the shooting hand is called a gooseneck.

The left hand does not add any power on a right-handed shot. It passively cradles the ball and then merely falls away during the shot. Many years ago, most shots were two-handed set shots, but it has long been understood that a one-handed shot is a higher percentage shot. The shooting hand does not snap back, but either gently follows through the shot

Shooting   27

FIGURE 2-6

THE GOOSENECK

The final position of the shooting hand is the *gooseneck*.

Here you see a common, but incorrect, post-shooting hand posture. The hand is reversed because the ball was shot with the little finger or outside part of the hand. The thumb is up, but should be down. The little finger is down, but should be up.

Notice how after the ball is flicked toward the hoop, the right hand holds the gooseneck position, while the left hand falls away from the ball.

in a downward arc, or is held relatively stationary for a moment. Either style is OK.

If your player does not properly flick the ball from the cradle, this can be remedied with some drills, particularly if you catch it early enough. Perhaps the best way for the child to change form is to shoot repeatedly against a high wall, and go through a few hundred wrist flicks, concentrating only on the form of the hand movement. A few such practice sessions will help make any correction needed. Good form is essential to shooting.

Aim at the Front of the Rim

Concentration is essential to good shooting, and the goal is to reduce any unnecessary movement, to be balanced and still. A shooter should aim to set the ball on or just beyond the front of the hoop. He should do this by focusing on the point of the hoop closest to him and setting the ball on top of that spot. This reduces the focus to a single point, instead of the whole space of the hoop. The shooter tries to loft the ball and set it down just on or past the point of the hoop closest to him.

Arcing the Ball Is Optimal

An arced ball has the best chance of scoring because it drops through the largest possible hoop opening. A lot of players shoot bricks, that is to say, balls that travel directly at the basket. These linear shots utilize a smaller window through the hoop than arced shots and therefore have less chance of scoring. A very high arc, however, is unnecessary, and lowers the percentage. For a comfortable arc, a good rule of thumb is to peak the arc at about 3 to 4 feet higher than the basket on a 15-foot shot. In close, a 1- to 2-foot arc is OK.

Follow the Shot

I think the toughest habit for a kid to break is that of standing immobile and watching the ball as it moves to the basket. A small but significant percentage of rebounds bounce back toward the shooter, and a player who moves to follow the shot to the basket will often get a rebound and a second chance. In shooting practice, tell the team to always take at least one or two steps forward following the shot, just to develop the habit. The habit of standing still and watching the ball is usually developed *during* shooting practice, and it's a bad one. Players should move to the hoop as they come down from the shot. In fact, it's good to land in front of the takeoff spot, leaning forward a tiny bit. The jump is straight up, with a slight forward tilt.

OK. Those are the mechanics of outside shooting. We have already covered some dynamics, such as taking the high percentage shot and getting the defender off balance, but there are a number of other dynamics to think about.

Look for the Open Player Underneath

An outside shooter may be good, but she'll never shoot more accurately than a player underneath the hoop. Also, remember that a fake shot is a great decoy and a good opportunity to pass to the big players underneath.

A good team player always looks for an open player with a better shot. That's how ball games are won—good percentage shooting.

Keep All Options Open

When faking, the idea isn't just to fake a dribble in order to shoot, or fake a shot in order to dribble; it's to do what the situation calls for. If the opponent takes the fake dribble, shoot. Sometimes, your player has to try several fakes before capitalizing on the one that works best. We discussed earlier the concept of *feeling* the defender's balance. Once he is off balance, go the other way.

Adjust the Shot If Necessary

Often the defender will recover and get a hand up in front of the shooter. Then the shooter must react or she will eat the ball. Sometimes it's enough to give the ball a bit more arc, enough to get over the hand, or perhaps to go for a bank shot, which adds both arc and a slight change in direction. Another solution is to double pump, that is, to withdraw the hand momentarily and restart the shot. Alternately, the player can fade away from the defender, and lean back to get more shooting angle and arc. React to the defender, relate to the defender, sense where she is at all times and take what opportunities are given.

A common error in shooting is to shoot the ball too far, past the rim. If this happens, chances are the forearm is too involved in pushing the ball. Have her use more wrist and less forearm.

Know Your Range and Shoot Confidently Within It

I'm not being negative when I tell kids to "know your range." Basketball is a team game. If a player hasn't spent the hours needed to shoot 15- to 19-foot shots, he can't practice them during a game. There is no individual right to shoot long shots.

Most players can and should take shots of 10 feet or less, if they can get the shot off without being blocked; but only players who have earned the long ones should ordinarily take them. We never say never, because there are times everyone should shoot a long shot, particularly when your players underneath have rebounding position.

A player learns through practice the range within which he makes most of his shots. Then there is a gray area, usually 10 to 15 feet. Finally, there is a range in which he misses most shots. Players should take open shots they can hit at least half of the time in practice.

When a player is within his effective range, he should be confident enough to take a good shot whenever he can. How often do we see a player refuse to take a simple 8-foot jumper because he lacks the confidence? Shoot those shots—even poor shooters will make a lot of the shorter ones. A player must *expect* the ball to go in the hoop when shooting within his range.

Of course, the best remedy for lack of confidence is simply more practice. As a coach you will use practice time mostly for teaching general dynamics and for conditioning. Shooting practice gets little time. You can tell the kids how to shoot, but you should expect them to practice on their own and with their parents. Kids who practice will get more playing time, because they will put numbers up on the scoreboard. Coaches keep statistics, such as number of points, rebounds, steals, assists, turnovers—they all count! The kids with the numbers will play. Some coaches don't know talent if they fall over it, but the numbers usually don't lie, and lineups are often made based on the numbers.

INSIDE SHOOTING—MECHANICS AND DYNAMICS

Basketball underneath the hoop is the tall person's turf. The highest percentage shooting, 70 percent or better, comes inside, underneath the hoop, or within 6 feet or so. It's the boiler room area of the court, where you'll find a lot of grunting, leaning, boxing out, shot blocking, rebounding, fancy lay-ups, slam dunks, hook shots and soft-touch jumpers, sometimes banked off the glass. It's the world of basketball at its best. Sure, the three-point shots have opened the game up, and a player with quick hands is valuable dribbling and stealing passes, but the game is still most exciting *in the paint*, the area between the foul lines (usually painted in a different color).

It's rare for a player to be successful underneath without at least average or above average height. Short quick players can sometimes zip past the big men and get a shot off if they are agile. Such players can visit, but not live, underneath. Big players get rebounds, block shots and score points under the hoop. If a player is short, it's not a problem, but he must learn to dribble, pass and shoot outside. Guide him in the direction appropriate to his size.

There are basically three inside shots: the driving lay-up, the chippie or short jump shot, and the hook.

The Lay-Up

A lay-up is still the most exciting shot in basketball, and it's also one of the simplest. Kids dream of Michael Jordan dribbling toward the basket, leaping and flying through the air, and spinning into a reverse slam dunk. My thirteen-year-old son regularly broke into this imaginary move in our

FIGURE 2-8

SHOOTING LAY-UPS

When *shooting a lay-up*, lift the entire right side—leg and arm—and jump straight up, driving off the left foot. Rotate the body for easier landing.

hallway, dunking into an imaginary basket! Well, young kids won't dunk for a while, but a drive and lay-up are certainly possible, and should be emphasized and perfected above all other forms of shooting.

The reason is simple. Outside shooting is tough. A kid has to shoot a few thousand shots before she can consistently hit the hoop. No problem, it just takes time. However, lay-ups can be learned more quickly. Although kids usually play pretty poorly on defense, an offensive player who can dribble a bit will be able to advance the ball up close for an inside shot. It looks good, and it will get a cheer from the fans. It will help the team, and your player will take a big step forward in development. Most importantly, it's easy to do and comes quickly with a little practice.

For young beginners, the scores are low. The players generally can't shoot outside (or inside). A kid who can drive a few steps to the hoop and shoot a lay-up will have the best chance of scoring in youth basketball. If you are a parent, teach your child to do lay-ups and, more quickly than with any other skill, her confidence will grow and with it the ball player within will emerge.

One of the themes I've taken in this book is confidence building, and this reflects my general approach to coaching. I believe it's good to get kids going, focus on something they can use right away, sort of jump-start the engine. Once a kid gets to a point where she can contribute to a team, confidence takes over and she will blossom like the yellow forsythia on the first warm spring day. Kids on a team will pass the ball to a player if they feel she can do something with it, otherwise they will tend to look for someone who can. This is why I emphasize dribbling so much. Here are the basics of shooting a lay-up:

Make a Move

A lay-up usually starts when the player gets the ball about 10 to 15 feet from the basket. If it's a designed play, such as a screen, then the player receives the ball on the run and continues to the hoop. More often, however, a player gets a pass or rebound and needs to make an individual move, that is, fake the defender. We have talked about fakes before, so I won't repeat it all here. The idea is to get the defender off balance, feint one way or fake a shot, and then drive (dribble) around him going the opposite way from the fake.

Claim the Lane and Explode Through It

Once a lane for dribbling is available, the player very quickly claims it. He can't dribble through a stationary defender, but he can claim any open lane. I always say to drive as close to the defender as possible. If he reacts and moves back into that lane, he will commit a foul. The official will usually call the foul on a moving defender. Encourage players to claim the lane and stick to it. It always helps to get the other team to foul: The idea is to pick a point just on the outside the defender's shoulder and drive your shoulder right by it. If the defender reaches in, he fouls. Otherwise, break to the hoop!

Keep Everything Low

Early in a driving lay-up, the player keeps shoulders down, elbows in, waist and knees bent, head up, and ball dribbled low to the floor. This helps quickness, increases ball control, and protects the ball. The player should take care not to bump the opponent, or lower the shoulder into him. Stay low and steady.

Take the Two Free Steps and Find an Opening

The last two steps of a shooting drive are the most important. They are free, that is, no dribble is required. (Actually, the first step comes off the last dribble and establishes the pivot; only one "free" step is technically allowed. Frankly, I can't figure out the Pro rules on this anymore; it seems that extra steps are OK as long as they look great!) These last two "giant" steps usually cover a fair bit of ground. Since your player is no longer dribbling, he has the opportunity to look up for an opening. The ball is held firmly in both hands and the player "feels" the defense. Usually, a big player underneath the hoop will react once you drive by the first defender, so everything must happen very quickly. The two giant steps are often enough to get to a spot where the ball can be laid-up to the basket.

A great drill for making this point is to have a child start at the foul line and make a lay-up with only one dribble! It's easily done, and it teaches the player how much distance he can cover without much dribbling. After practicing a while, have him do it from farther out, with only one dribble.

The best angle to take is 45° to the hoop. Obviously, there is often no choice. If there is, come in at this angle since it maximizes ball control and use of the backboard.

Get the Proper Footwork

Pump up the knee on the same side as the shooting hand and drive straight up with the opposite foot. Kids often push off the wrong foot, and it's important right away to get the proper footwork. If the lay-up is right-handed, then the right arm needs to stretch up, and the whole right side should lift with it. Raising the right knee high does this. The concept is to raise the whole right side on right-handed shots (vice versa for lefty lay-ups). It comes after a few practice sessions. Note this means that, coming off the dribble, the first free step for a righty lay-up is with the right foot.

At the beginning of that step, the player grabs the ball with both hands and prepares to shoot, finally driving off the left foot. Lifting the right knee also adds to the height of the jump. Finally, the player needs to remember to jump straight up. This not only adds to the height of the jump, but it also slows down the forward movement of the body so the ball hits the backboard a bit more softly.

Use the Backboard

Pick a spot and lay the ball up softly off the glass. Because the overwhelming majority of lay-ups are shot off the backboard, you should teach even your youngest players to use it for this shot. The hardest thing about shooting lay-ups is controlling the speed of the ball bouncing off the backboard. Most missed shots arise because the ball hits the backboard too hard as a result of the body's forward speed and momentum. Jumping straight up slows the ball a bit, but it still needs to be laid-up softly.

The ball sits in the right hand, palm turned partially inward toward the shooter. The shot can be done with the palm outward, like a jump shot, but it's much tougher to control the ball speed. The hand must soften the ball's impact upon the backboard to adjust for the forward motion of the body. This is done by flipping the ball backward a bit to decrease its speed. As a player becomes experienced, spin may be applied to compensate for odd angles.

The backboards are usually marked with a square, and the player lays the ball up against the lines of the square. Teach the team to find the right spot and hit it every time: With practice, a player will shoot automatically and not need to focus on the square.

Next, the body rotates or twists counterclockwise a bit to prepare for a controlled landing. This rotation should be coached, but don't confuse things too much in the early stages. Just tell your child to twist a bit in order to land on balance.

Dish the Ball Off If Needed

We mentioned that once the ball handler successfully passes a defender, a big player underneath will react to defend his teammate. If this happens, the defender has abandoned, and opened up, the man he was guarding. Your player continues with the lay-up, inciting the big defender to commit fully, and then dishes (passes) the ball off to the open player. It works like a charm!

Practice the Lefty Shot

Be patient here since, for righties, developing a lefty lay-up is the toughest thing in basketball. Start slowly. Urge your players to try it a few times. It will feel very awkward, and will progress slowly. To execute a lefty shot, reverse the footwork. On the left side of the basket, a lefty shot is more effective since it places the body between the defender and the ball. That's why all your players should be comfortable doing it.

Be Fancy in Practice

Some coaches discourage kids from shooting trick or fancy off-balance lay-ups during practice, but I never did. In a game the defender usually doesn't allow a textbook shot, so the shooter often needs to contort a bit. Therefore, this situation should be practiced. Let the kids have fun with it once in a while. Use the hang time, the air time, to double pump, twist and change angles.

Short Jump Shots and Chippies

Short jump shots and chippies get blocked most often, because they are shot in close to the hoop where the big players roam and they don't have the advantage of body motion which a lay-up provides.

The mechanics of short shots are similar to those of longer outside shots except that you need to be much more concerned about the defender. The shot needs to be carried out very quickly, with quick moves and quick release.

Fakes are even more important in close to the hoop. The best fake is to raise the ball quickly as if to shoot, get the defender to jump, and then go up as she comes down. Sometimes, a few fake pumps with the ball are needed to get the defender to react.

Often a short jump shot can effectively use the backboard. It's a bit tougher, but it provides a higher, off-line arc, which is harder to defend. Ordinarily, any shot within 4 to 5 feet of the hoop and to the side should use the backboard. Jumpers in front of the hoop go directly to the rim. Remind your player to focus on the point of the rim closest to her and to arc the ball softly to that spot. A dish off to an open player can also be a very effective option.

The Hook Shot

The hook shot is pretty much a big player's shot, because it is used underneath the hoop. Usually, the shot occurs when an outside player passes to the shooter, whose back is initially to the hoop. The shooter turns sideways to the hoop, fakes a turn one way, usually with the head and shoulders, then leans the other way, turning off the right foot (for a righty hook) and jumping with strength from the left foot (or hopping and jumping off both feet). The legs should feel balanced. If the defender is moving, lean into her.

In preparation to shoot, bring the ball up the right side of the body, hold it tightly, then raise it with the right hand away from the defender, protecting it with the other forearm and the other side of the body. Focus on the closest point of the hoop; look at it specifically, then flick the ball over it softly. Hook shots do not use the backboard. The key here is jumping aggressively and looking at the nearest point on the rim. A big player must develop a hook shot. It's tough to defend, and can be very accurate if practiced. Like all shots, it should be practiced every time you play. (See Figure 2-9.)

Foul Shots

Foul shots certainly deserve special mention. It can be said that foul shooting wins or loses most close games, and this is so at all levels of play. At

FIGURE 2-9

HOOK SHOT

Underneath the hoop, the hook is an essential shot.

youth ages, good foul shooting is rare, but since scores are usually low, a foul shooter can win a game.

Players get two free shots if fouled in the act of shooting and the shot is missed. Two shots are also awarded for any intentional or flagrant foul. One shot and possession of the ball is awarded for technical fouls, such as excessive shouting by the coach, foul language, or unsportsmanlike conduct. If fouled in any other manner, a player gets to shoot only if the other team has accumulated five personal fouls during the half. In these cases, one foul shot is awarded, and a second bonus shot is awarded if the first shot scores. This is called a one-and-one.

In lining up for foul shots, two defenders take the positions closest to the hoop, between the block and the first lane markers, on both sides of the lane. Two of the shooter's teammates line up next, followed by two defenders. The remaining defender and an opponent usually line up near mid-court to prepare for a defensive rebound and subsequent play toward the other end of the court. The fifth offensive player usually hovers in the wing area.

Players may enter the foul lane after the ball leaves the shooter's hand, but the shooter can't enter the lane until the ball touches the rim or backboard.

Shooting foul shots is much like shooting jump shots, except the feet don't leave the ground. In the old days, players like the great Wilt Chamberlain used to shoot fouls underhanded with two hands. However, the highest percentage shots, as said before, are one-handed flicks from a cradle. The ball is brought over the head, cradled and shot with one hand. The shooting hand ends up in a gooseneck, just as with jump shots. The head and shoulders are square to the hoop. The shooting elbow points at the hoop.

Much of foul shooting comes from the legs. They must bend and extend into the shot. The body starts low and fully extends, up on the toes, and the player stays up on the toes while the ball is in flight. *The key is to stay extended into the shot.*

It's also important to point the front foot, usually the right foot for a righty shot, at the hoop. Don't let it turn in because that will retard full extension. The other foot can be back a comfortable distance. Remember, as with all shooting, shoot with the legs. It's also good to make sure the hands are dry, and shake any tenseness out of the wrists and fingers.

Foul shots should be practiced, preferably a minimum of twenty-five, at the end of each practice session, while the player is tired. Shooting while tired simulates game conditions.

Shooting Drills

The best way to practice shooting is just to do it! The great shooters practiced for hours a day as kids. Get the mechanics working properly and then shoot thousands of shots. Kids won't get to practice shooting much at team practices, as I said, so they have to do it on their own. This is where the parent can be most helpful. A parent can rebound and feed the pass back to his or her child for another shot, doing many repetitions in a relatively short time. I did this for a summer once with my older son and his shot accuracy improved dramatically. After a while, the parent should put a little pressure on the child as he shoots by going back for the rebound. The child can fake and drive, while the parent applies enough pressure to make it challenging, but not overwhelming.

FIGURE 2-11
FEEDING REBOUNDS

Probably the most helpful and easiest practice a parent can provide is to feed her child rebounds.

Ultimately, a game of one-on-one is great practice. I used to defend against my son at nine years old, and I would not use my hands to defend his shots (my head was about as high as a kid's hand and supplied sufficient pressure). I also would not raise my hands above my head to rebound—it kept things more even.

Feeding Passes
Feeding passes for shots is the best practice. The parent should remind the child to point her elbow, cradle, flick the wrist, use soft hands, keep her eyes on the front of the rim (the point of the rim closest to the child), keep the head and shoulders square, shoot quickly, release quickly, jump higher, fake the dribble, follow up the shot, shoot with confidence, shoot from the legs, feel graceful. After a while, the parent will chase far fewer rebounds! (See Figure 2-11.)

Form Drills
There are several form drills which can be employed early in the season. Coaches should practice the triple-threat stance in conjunction with these drills.

Wall Drill
Players line up along a wall and practice jump shooting form. They jump as high as they can, cradle and gooseneck flick the ball with the wrist.

They should start from a certain spot on the floor and ensure that they land at the same spot. They get the rebound, get set and shoot again. Use the checklist at the end of the book to spot defects in their form.

21 Jumper
This drill practices shooting and following up shots. Two teams of two players each are positioned for 15-foot jump shots. A player on each team shoots, follows up for the rebound, and passes back to his teammate who in turn shoots and rebounds. This continues until a team gets 21 points (one for each shot). Teams call out their score with each shot.

21 Lay-Up
This drill is like 21 Jumper except the players drive from beyond the foul line and do lay-ups. After rebounding, the player passes to his teammate and runs to the opposite side of the basket from which he just shot to await his turn. This ensures he will alternate righty and lefty lay-ups. Lay-ups done from the left side must be shot lefty. You might stand under the hoop to ensure that players jump straight up. You can also apply some pressure and even jostle the players a bit to simulate game conditions under the hoop, and to encourage a firm ball grip.

Run and Jump
This drills for jump shots from a dribble. Guards line up in the middle of the half-court line and forwards line up along the sideline 20 feet from the end line. Guards dribble to any point 15 feet from the hoop, stop quickly and jump shoot. Forwards dribble toward the corner and do the same. This drill can also be done along a 15-foot semicircle, but make sure players dribble a few times before shooting. Players must follow the shot and get their own rebound. You can place defenders along the inside of this perimeter to apply light defense.

Fifty Freebies
Players should try to make at least 50 foul shots a day; a hundred is better. Two players take turns shooting, ten shots at a time. Keep shooting until 50 are made. At younger ages adjust the number desired. The other player rebounds and then shoots when it's his or her turn.

Tapping Drill
Position two players under either side of the hoop. One throws the ball off the backboard or rim for the other to tap in. Then the second player throws it up for the first player to tap in. Switch sides after a while.

Chapter Three

DRIBBLING

The most important skill in youth basketball is dribbling, so it follows that the most important thing you can do as coach is to teach and emphasize this. How often do we see a youngster out on a basketball playground, standing there shooting, just shooting and nothing else?

Sure, shooting is very important. Passing is even more important to team success. However, dribbling is a purely individual skill, and it is the most important initial step in the development of a young basketball player. It is definitely the best confidence builder. A boy or girl who can move with the basketball will be valuable to the team, and also will be able to develop other skills more quickly.

THE IMPORTANCE OF DRIBBLING FOR BEGINNERS

Children typically begin playing basketball in clinic-type programs for a few years prior to fifth or sixth grade when regular traveling teams are formed. Observe these programs and you'll quickly notice that confusion reigns on the court. Few shots are taken because the ball is constantly being stolen. A child will get the ball and just freeze. He will be immediately surrounded by opposing players, and will either throw the ball away or have it swiped from his hands.

The standout on the floor is the child who does not freeze, but who can dribble the ball around the other players. This child can then advance for a good shot, or pass the ball to an open teammate. Thus, confidence grows, all skills become developed, and a basketball player emerges. Dribbling is the ticket! When children lack this skill, they are somewhat afraid of the ball. You can see they don't want the ball, and they lack confidence when they have it. Practice dribbling to address this problem and the result will be a bounty of self-assurance.

So, get your player to work on dribbling and handling the ball, both during team practice and at home. When my youngest son was eight years old, I cleared out a small area in the basement (it's cold outside during basketball season in New Jersey), a space of about $10' \times 10'$, but even a smaller space would have been OK. He would go down for 20 minutes

FIGURE 3-1
PRACTICE DRIBBLING

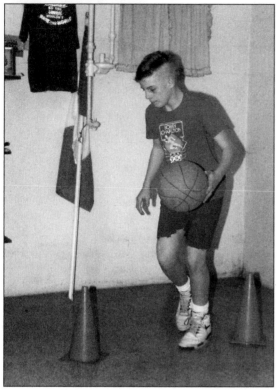

Practicing in the cellar is a ticket to great progress.

and practice dribbling. I told him to make sudden moves, perform figure eights, dribble behind the back, set up obstacles and dribble around them, and also practice dribbling with both hands. After a while, I would put some pressure on him, try to steal the ball. We set up a runway between cellar rooms so he would get some speed for a 20-foot speed dribble. In a very short time he improved significantly, and the improvement was quite noticeable as he played in the clinic. Don't expect miracles; expect improvement! It will come.

On warmer days, we would go outside. Any hard, flat surface is OK: streets (watch the cars), sidewalks, driveway. It's not necessary to have a basket to practice dribbling! Have your son or daughter start by dribbling, back and forth, over a 50-foot distance, right-handed one way, left-handed coming back. It works! Tell parents of your players to urge this to their children.

FIGURE 3-2
DRIBBLE WITH THE FINGERS

Step 1. *Dribbling* is done with the fingers and the upper palm.

Step 2. The ball is kept out on the fingers as much as possible.

HOW TO DRIBBLE

Here are the seven key aspects of good dribbling.

Finger Control—The ball is dribbled with the fingers, particularly the thumb and the three middle fingers. Some kids initially use the palm of the hand. However, the palm has only a limited role in helping the fingers to receive and cradle the ball. The fingers do most of the work. You want the ball out on the fingers and the upper palm near the fingers as much as possible. (See Figure 3-2.) The upper palm and lower thumb area often receive the bounced ball, especially if the player is on the run, but then the fingertips take over. They direct the downward dribble as the ball rolls off the fingertips.

Receive, Cradle and Pump—When little kids start dribbling for the first time, their natural impulse is to *strike* the ball downward when dribbling. The hand should not strike the ball, rather it reaches for, then softens and receives it well before the top of its bounce, cradles it for a split second, and then pumps it back to the floor. The hand actually withdraws as it meets the ball, so it catches the ball, controls it and then directs it down again. The idea is to maximize the amount of time the hand is in contact with the ball, thereby allowing for greater control. Often in dribbling the player needs to make sudden moves or change speeds. The hand needs to have sufficient contact and control so that these moves can be made. It helps the player be able to send the ball back out in the direction desired with appropriate velocity. (See Figure 3-3.)

The point of contact between the hand and the ball varies, depending on the direction the player takes. Usually, the index and middle fingers are on top of the ball, with the fingertips at or just forward of the upper-most point of the ball's curve. However, if the player is running with the ball, the fingers make contact farther back from the top center so they can push the ball forward. If a left turn is needed, then the fingers will cradle the ball more from the right side. In the past, rules against cradling the ball from underneath, called carrying or palming, were stricter. Fouls for palming, in which the palm and fingers completely control direction, are rarely called any more in the pros, unless the violation is flagrant.

Move With Rhythm—In order to dribble well, the entire arm and shoulder move in a pumping action, rising at the shoulder and bending at the elbow. The concept you want to teach is one of rhythm. The arm pumps in rhythm with the ball's bouncing. This rhythm is the essence of dribbling.

First, get your players to understand the rhythm between the pumping action of the arm and the ball's bouncing. Get them to think about that rhythm while practicing. During a game they won't have time to think about it, but if they practice regularly, it will become natural.

The next step is to get the entire body moving in the same rhythm, that is, hook the feet into the pumping of the arm and the bouncing of the ball. The concept is the same: The entire body must move in the same rhythm.

A good drill for developing rhythm is the *stutter step*. Have your players spread their legs, left foot forward, and move forward with a small hopping or stutter step, in rhythm with the ball. The left foot is always forward

FIGURE 3-3

RECEIVE, CRADLE AND PUMP

Step 1. The steps to good dribbling are *receive*, *cradle* and *pump*. The player's fingers extend to receive the ball.

Step 2. The fingertips receive it and begin to withdraw.

Step 3. The hand withdraws, cradling the ball at the top of the bounce.

Step 4. The hand pumps the ball back down.

when dribbling righty, but small steps are taken, pushing off the back foot. This drill builds the sense of rhythm so essential to good dribbling. I tell my kids to remember the movie *Rocky III* when Apollo taught Rocky how to get rhythm. He used a stutter step too! If your child practices in the cellar, turn on a radio and have her dribble-dance to the beat of the music.

Develop Both Hands—If a player can dribble with only one hand, his ability to move will always be limited. Defenders usually lean to the left a bit to cut off the space to the dribbler's right. The ability to then switch to the left hand and drive to the left side opens a whole new dimension and substantially improves a player's offensive potential. You need to continually remind your players to use both hands. Don't nag, just encourage them to devote some time for the other hand. Use drills to get them started.

If a player is a righty, have him spend time using only the left hand. When you apply pressure to his right side, be sure he attempts the left-handed drive. It will be difficult, sloppy, and awkward for him at first, so be supportive. Remind him that he will improve; praise the first sign of improvement. Remind him how hard it seemed to learn to whistle or ride a bike at first, and how easy it was once he got the hang of it.

Head Up, Eyes Front—A child initially dribbles with her head down, keeping the ball in her field of vision. As she improves and develops a feel for the ball and its rhythm, she will be able to direct her attention more to what's going on around her. To the extent she keeps her head down, she will be unaware of opportunities around her: Who is open for a pass, what lane is available for advancing the ball, which way is the defender leaning, what opportunities are developing from the flow of play?

I wouldn't harp on this too much. The head will come up as the player becomes experienced enough to know where the ball is by feel instead of by sight. You need to talk about the concept and why it's helpful to be able to focus on the whole floor. There are practice techniques which can help, such as closing the eyes while dribbling in order to force more reliance on feeling the ball's motion. Patience is needed here since much practice is required before the feel of the ball is sufficiently developed. It is useful however to quietly remind your players, every once in a while, to try to lift their attention, to be more broadly aware of what's going on around them.

FIGURE 3-7

DRIBBLE LOW

Low dribbles are hard to steal and much easier to control.

Keep Everything Low—Keep the ball low in traffic, the body balanced and relaxed. A high bouncing dribble is easy to steal in traffic. Also, the longer the ball is away from the hand, the fewer the opportunities to change direction or react quickly. During practice, and especially during drills, remind your players to keep the ball, the dribbling hand, the dribbling elbow and the center of gravity of the body low.

Practice keeping the dribble at knee height. Have them observe and feel the differences between a high and low dribble. In a low dribble, the tempo and rhythm are much faster and the ball is more under control. (See Figure 3-7.)

The body should always feel balanced and graceful, weight forward on the balls of the feet. Staying in touch with the rhythm of the ball and staying relaxed help greatly. The great players make it look effortless because they are balanced, relaxed, in touch with the ball and confident in their ability.

For speed dribbling, the ball bounces much higher. The hand pushes

FIGURE 3-8

SHIELD THE BALL WITH THE BODY

A player should use her shoulder to shield the ball, but be careful not to foul the defender.

the ball out in front, just a bit to the side. High dribbles are for speed; low dribbles to maintain possession.

Shield the Ball—Keep the body between the ball and the defender. This is also called shielding. The defender can't get to the ball without fouling if the dribbler keeps her body between the defender and the ball. Again, this is more easily done if she can dribble with both hands. While the dribbling elbow is in close, the other elbow is out shielding the body (as long as she doesn't push with it). (See Figure 3-8.)

PIVOTS, FAKES AND FEINTS

Often a player will receive a pass on the run, such as a mid-court pass, the final pass in a give and go play and other passes to a player cutting toward the basket. In these situations she should continue to use her momentum and speed to its best advantage. If there is a free lane in front

FIGURE 3-9

THE PIVOT

Step 1. The *pivot rule* lets the ball handler rotate 180° on her toes in order to get the defender behind her. As the defender approaches, the ball handler first establishes the left foot as the pivot.

Step 2. To protect the ball, the ball handler pivots counterclockwise on the left toes, away from the defender.

of the player, it's almost always best to move directly through it and advance the ball. Often, however, a player will receive a pass while closely guarded. This requires her to put a move on the defender, get the defender to lean or commit to one side, and then quickly dribble the other way while the defender is off balance. This is done by faking to one side and going to the opposite.

The Pivot

Before further discussing the specifics of faking, we need to consider the concept of the pivot. For some reason, kids tend to learn the concept slowly and this severely limits their range of opportunity. They feel that their feet can move only while dribbling. The pivot rule, however, allows a player to pivot freely on one foot. The toes of the pivot foot cannot leave the floor and cannot slide, but they can rotate as much as needed and the heel may leave the floor. A player closely guarded by a defender can pivot 180° in order to get the defender behind her, thus protecting the ball. (See Figure 3-9.) A pivot can be part of a fake, stepping sharply in one direction to get a defender off balance and then pivoting back the other direction.

Fakes

There are several types of fakes. Keep in mind most fakes require the player be able to dribble with both hands. Once a defender knows your player can dribble only to one side, then any fakes to the other side are not effective.

FIGURE 3-10

FULL BODY FAKE

Step 1. The *full body fake* requires a sharp step to the left with the entire body.

Step 2. The ball handler then drives to the opposite side, close to the defender.

Body Fake

The most common fake is a *full body fake*. Here, using the right foot as a pivot, the player steps sharply toward the left, bringing the body and ball to the left. He then pivots quickly back to the right, driving off the pivot foot. (See Figure 3-10.) The idea behind any fake is to get the defender to believe you will move one way so he follows you. I find it useful to teach the kids to think they are actually pulling the defender off balance, and then suddenly change direction. The direction change must be very quick in order to dart through the lane opened by the fake. Tell your players to drive right by the defender and aggressively step into and claim the lane, leaving only inches away from the defender. If the defender comes back, he will commit a foul.

The *head, shoulder* or *ball fake* is a variation of the fuller fake. The idea is to fake the head, the shoulder, the ball or any combination of these three, just to get the defender to hesitate and then very quickly snap back the other way.

The *double fake* includes a halfhearted fake one way and a full intensive fake the other. If the defender thinks he has picked up the first fake and goes the other way, your player should head in the direction of the first fake. The idea is not so much to plan a series of fakes, but rather to feel the defender's balance and take advantage of the first mistake he makes.

The *shot* or *pass fake* is probably the most effective fake in basketball. The player pretends to take a set or jump shot (but the pivot foot does not leave the ground) and then, as the defender comes forward or jumps to defend the shot, simply dribbles around him. Young players fall for this often! It's important to look at the basket and really pretend to shoot to get the defender to come forward. Sometimes the player may only need to raise the ball quickly to get a defender to react. Similarly, a player may pretend to pass the ball to a teammate, hoping the defender will lean toward the pass, and then dribble the opposite way.

Feint or Change of Pace

Another effective fake is a change in speed while dribbling. The player pretends to speed up with a big explosive step and then slows down suddenly. Often the defender will be caught off balance. Any change in speed while dribbling can be quite effective in unbalancing a defender.

DRIBBLING DRILLS

We've touched on a couple of drills already in this chapter. The important idea in dribbling is just to do it and keep doing it. Much can be done at home, since dribbling practice needs only a hard surface. In cold weather, players can practice in the basement on a concrete floor; in warmer weather, on the driveway or sidewalk. Practice can include just fooling around with the ball, switching hands, sudden movements (behind the back, between the legs), and speed dribbling; use both hands, use two balls, close the eyes, practice fakes.

Parents can help during at-home practice sessions by creating pressure situations: Stand as an obstacle for a child to dribble around, or attempt to steal the ball. Apply enough pressure to make it a challenge, but don't dominate. Win a few, lose a few. Make it fun!

Cone Drill—Set up a half dozen or more cones in a line about 4 to 6 feet apart and have players dribble, weaving through the cones. When a player gets to the end, she speed dribbles back. Then start over again. Use a stopwatch or a watch with a second hand to measure the best time and then have them run against the clock. (See Figure 3-12.) Have players do a series, switching the ball from right- to left-handed dribbling.

One-On-One—Let your players start at the top of the key, dribbling against you or another coach. Have her put a fake on you as you defend, and then drive toward the basket for a lay-up. Apply light pressure.

FIGURE 3-12
CONE DRIBBLING

Cone dribbling is a great drill that requires players to dribble while weaving through the cones. Players can be timed, and can also practice switching hands while dribbling.

Keep-Away—Two players stay inside a 10-foot square. One dribbles. One tries to get the ball. This drill teaches how to use the body to shield the ball.

King of the Hill—Several players dribble in a square area and try to tap each other's ball away, with one hand, while dribbling with the other. The last one "alive" wins.

Dribble Race—Divide players into two or three teams which form lines at one end of the court. The lead player in each line must dribble-race to the other end and return, handing the ball to the next in line who then repeats the sprint-dribble. Do the second race left-handed. Losers get 15 pushups.

Chapter Four

PASSING

Nothing is more important to team play than good, snappy passing. A child will play less if he tends to throw the ball away, so he must learn the importance of snappy pass work. A bad pass causes the receiver to lose momentum and usually results in a lost shooting opportunity or a turnover, that is, losing the ball to the opponent.

A good pass can set up an easy shot. As stated in the second chapter, kids often just want to go out and shoot, shoot, shoot. I have no problem with shooting, as long as it is put in perspective and other skills are also developed. Good dribbling and good passing lead to good shots. The great ball players—Bob Cousy, Magic Johnson, Larry Bird—were better known for their incredible passing ability than for shooting. As I look back at my own playing days under the hoop, the times I scored a lot occurred when my team had a really good passing guard. His passes gave me easy shots underneath, so he made me look good.

PASSING IN YOUTH BALL

Unfortunately, passing is the nemesis of youth basketball. It is a team skill, so it requires "two to tango." If either the passer or the receiver makes a mistake, the ball can easily be lost to the opposing team. At the very young ages, passing is quite bad and confusion reigns. In most clinics, players are not allowed to press; that is, they must allow the opposing team to move the ball past the mid-court line before they can defend or try to steal. Were it not for such a rule, the kids would rarely get the ball very far up court.

Actually, the biggest problem with passing in youth basketball is inexperience and the lack of confidence that inexperience brings. A kid gets the ball and freezes. He feels awkward and clumsy. Opposing players take advantage of the hesitation and close in on him. He does not know how to dribble out of it. He panics a bit, closes off his awareness of his teammates and doesn't see them for a pass. Often, the player will just pivot, turn his back to the defender and cover up! As a result, the ball is stolen from his hands or an opponent gets a hand on the ball and a jump ball is called. If he is closely guarded and holds the ball for more than five seconds, he loses the ball on a five-second violation. Another result may be that he just makes a bad pass. Chances are you will see some of your players in this situation. If you do, relax, it is common. It occurs because they have not played enough. Make sure you tell them this, and suggest they resolve to work a bit harder to improve basic skills.

FIXING THE PASSING PROBLEM

There is no quick cure to this problem. Dribbling practice will allow the player to dribble out of jams, keep her head up and open her focus or attention to the whole floor, as stated in chapter three. Once a player has stopped dribbling, the pivot moves will very effectively protect the ball and buy time to spot an open teammate for a pass. The pivot should not be just a cover-up, however, and it is preferable to face the defender strongly, fake him and dribble or pass around him. As coach, you can teach the kids plays based on prearranged patterns of movement, the main idea of which is to get a player open for a pass and an easy shot. It helps to know ahead of time where teammates are supposed to be and thereby anticipate where the pass should go. Eventually, as players play together for a time, they begin to know each other's moves.

You need to be patient here. Good passing can only be developed with experience. It's important to teach your players to look for the open teammate. Ball-hogs don't last long in basketball. No matter how good they are, they are not good for the team if they won't pass. Teammates eventually retaliate and won't give the ball to a ball-hog. It always leads to trouble. If a player gets this way, you must try to help change his approach. It's not enough that he is better than the other kids, if that is indeed true. You must help him understand that only team players survive the long run.

On the other hand, there are some kids who always pass. They don't try to dribble; they never try to shoot. They just don't want the ball! If a child falls into this pattern, don't be alarmed. Many kids do. However, you need to build up his confidence. Words are helpful, but they are empty unless he regularly practices ball handling skills.

There is no quick fix for any passing problem! But regular practice will definitely result in improvement. You need to believe this if your players are to believe it. I live right next to an outdoor basketball court, and over the years I have seen various children from the neighborhood on the court. The ones who show up most often improve and become decent ball players. Pretty soon, they are varsity high school players. It's as simple as that! Practice and repetition work. One need not be "born with it." It's like learning how to type. It seems impossible at first, but with practice and experience it becomes second nature. It can be learned. So can basketball skills!

PASSING TECHNIQUES

When it comes to passing, setting up a *good* pass is key. Good passing is less a technical skill and more the result of good individual or team dynamics. There are, however, some basic techniques for passing and receiving the ball.

Use Two Hands

A basketball is pretty big; it's tough to control with only one hand. The activity on the court is fast and furious and full of sudden movements. Nearly all short or mid-range passes are two-handed, and the main reason for this is to control the ball as it is passed. A one-handed pass can roll off the hand as it is thrown. Control it with two hands.

A more important reason to use two hands is that passes must happen very quickly. The ball is usually already in front of the body, and there is no time to wind up for a one-handed pass. The ball is passed from the front of the torso, and the second hand is needed to give strength and power to the pass.

Obviously, a full-court pass needs the full power of an extended arm and must be thrown like a baseball. Otherwise, use both hands. (See Figure 4-1.)

Use Proper Hand Position

Spread fingers and rotate up toward chest area. Holding the ball at its sides, spread the thumb and index finger to form an oval with each other. The other fingers are spread at a relaxed distance from each other, not too far. This hand position maximizes both control of the ball and power coming through the fingers.

When a ball is caught or taken up from the dribbling position the hands are on the side, fingers out and thumbs up; and the ball is usually waist high. The passing motion begins by bringing the hands up and back to the chest. The fingers rotate upward and a bit back toward the upper chest as far as is comfortable. When the hands rotate, the elbows lift a bit to get more shoulder strength into the ball. The farther the hands rotate, the more power can be placed on the ball as the fingers snap or whip outward.

FIGURE 4-1

TWO-HAND CHEST PASS

Step 1. The *two-hand chest pass* gives your player maximum control of the ball. First, form an oval with the thumbs and index fingers.

Step 2. Rotate the ball and fingertips up and into the chest area, to ensure power in the pass.

Step 3. Drive the ball straight out in a whipping action as the ball rolls off the fingers and flick the wrists outward.

The ball is passed from in close to the chest for maximum power. The chest moves forward and down as the player steps toward the target.

Step Toward the Target

This action helps both accuracy and power, getting the body in motion with the pass. It must be a very quick step, however, in order to signal the pass and alert the defense to try to steal. Add power and accuracy by moving toward the target as much as possible. (See Figure 4-2.)

FIGURE 4-2

STEP INTO THE TARGET

A strong and quick step toward the target adds power and increases control.

Drive Forward

Drive body and hands forward and snap the wrists and fingers outward. This is all one movement. Drive the ball directly outward in a straight line. Power is transmitted to the pass from the whipping action of the wrists as the ball rolls off the fingers, principally the index finger. The index finger is the center of the pass, and is the last finger to touch the ball. Stay on the balls of the feet.

Stress Passing Techniques

Remind your player of these passing techniques as you have a catch or as she passes the ball off a wall. (As a child, I used my cellar wall.) Have her think about her hand position as she catches the ball and then passes it. Have her notice how far back she rotates the hands, and how much more power comes with a greater rotation. Have her notice how much accuracy she gets from stepping toward the target, and the power she gets from driving with the back leg. Tell her to bend forward at the waist for even more power. If she gets the idea of the various building blocks of passing, she will naturally begin to use them. Your job is to make her aware of them and to help her practice them. Even if she is an advanced player, there is no more useful practice than a review of basics and mechanics.

THE DYNAMICS OF PASSING

Now that we have the techniques of chest passing covered, let's talk a bit about other aspects of the successful pass.

Passes Must Be Quick and Snappy—The key to successful passing is to get the ball to the receiver before it can be stolen. Passes must be quick and snappy. When drilling passes, you must insist on this.

Pass to an Open Space—The idea is to pass to the space toward which the receiver is moving. A pass directly to a player will slow her down, or lead to a lost ball if fumbled. If a player looks at the floor for a second, she will easily see any open space beneath the hoop: This is the best avenue for penetration.

Don't Broadcast the Pass—Good defenders have a knack for anticipating when to intercept passes. The worst thing to do on offense, then, is to look right at the target before a pass. You might as well just pass to the defender. The defender knows when his man is open for a pass; he just doesn't know when it's coming. Don't tell him in advance.

After playing a while—it doesn't take long—players develop what is called *floor vision*. They can see what's going on in front of them without having to focus on any one player. So they can see an open teammate without really looking at him. Since they never focus directly on the receiver, the defensive player is not tipped off. Sometimes, a good passer sees his target and then looks at another player while passing to the first target. This ability is quite valuable since it gets defenders off balance.

Lead the Receiver; Use His Momentum—If a player is cutting toward the basket, don't slow him down by passing behind him. If a player passes directly at him, by the time the ball arrives he will already be past it. So the player must pass to slightly in front of where the receiver is. Judge the speed of the receiver and pass the ball to meet him. Pass to open space.

Hit Receivers in the Chest—This is not a hard-and-fast rule. You actually want to get the ball to the receiver's hands. However, it's usually easiest to catch a ball about chest high, and players are supposed to keep their hands up anyway, so in front of the chest is where the hands should be. Obviously, don't throw at his head if his hands are at his waist! If his hands

FIGURE 4-4
LEAD THE RECEIVER—AWAY FROM THE DEFENDER

A player should pass the ball to the open space in front of her receiver, so the receiver gets the pass on the run, while moving away from the defender.

are down, a bounce pass is good. If a receiver is under the hoop, a high pass is more effective, since the player does not need to spend time bringing the ball up. Where the ball needs to be thrown varies, but chest high is the best rule of thumb.

Throw Away From the Defender—If a defender is on the right side of the offensive player's target, the pass should be made to the receiver's left so she can use her body to shield the ball. Often the receiver will have a hand up to indicate where she wants the ball, and that's the target. Again, an essential concept of passing is to pass to an open space allowing the receiver to get the pass on the run. (See Figure 4-4.)

TYPES OF PASSES

The two-handed chest pass I've described is used in the great majority of situations. However, at times other passes may be needed.

Bounce Passes

These passes are good in close situations, when the traffic is heavy. The bounce pass helps to get the ball down under the defender's hands. One problem with the bounce pass is the floor slows the ball down. Also, this

FIGURE 4-5

OVERHEAD AND BASEBALL PASS

For the *overhead pass*, extend the arms overhead and quickly snap the ball to the receiver.

The *baseball pass* is useful for very long passes, such as across or down court.

pass needs to be caught fairly low, which is not usually desirable. Use it only when needed to get the ball under and past a defender. Top spin helps speed the ball up after it bounces.

Overhead Pass

The two-hand overhead pass is commonly used to get a pass over the head of a defender. It is a very effective pass and is also a good pass fake. The pass is made with a quick inward flick of the wrists and a short step toward the receiver, and is used often after a rebound to the outlet. The player holds the ball high over her head, arms fully extended. Her body snaps forward at the waist, and her shoulders snap forward as well. (See Figure 4-5.)

Baseball Pass

The baseball pass is a one-handed throw, like throwing a baseball. It's used primarily for very long passes, usually as part of a fast break or to break a press. At very young ages, it is not used often since it's rather hard to catch; and the rules often do not allow it. (See Figure 4-5.)

Fake-Shot Pass

One of the most effective passes in basketball follows a fake jump shot. Just as the player is poised at the top of his jump, ready to shoot, he passes off to a teammate underneath. The defenders are caught off balance, expecting the shot and beginning to jockey for a possible rebound. The fake-shot pass serves to ensure that the ball gets to the receiver untouched, since defenders don't expect it; and it buys the receiver some time to get the shot off. The only problem is that sometimes this fakes out the receiver, and he misses the pass too! Make sure your players are always alert and ready to receive the ball.

RECEIVING PASSES

The art of passing is mainly in the pass itself. Receiving the pass is not complicated. However, many passes are not caught or are bobbled. These situations are preventable.

Know Where the Ball Is and Want It

The most important skill in receiving the pass is simply being alert. Herein lies the greatest difference between the decent ball player and the poor one. You must always expect the ball! Look at any youth basketball game and you will see that some kids get a lot of loose balls and rebounds and others don't. Some kids seem to never be looking when the ball is passed to them. Some kids never have the ball passed to them because they are not looking and they don't make eye contact with the passer. These kids don't seem to want the ball.

Players should never turn their backs to the ball, unless it's part of a play. They must always know where the ball is, and keep it in their field of vision. Most importantly, they should always be prepared to receive a pass, always be looking for the ball—they've got to want it. This is the key!

Kids who want the ball are easy to pick out. They play more aggressively. They are constantly trying to get into position for a pass. Their eyes are on the passer, searching to see if she will pass the ball, signaling they are ready for it with a hand up as a target. They dive for loose balls.

Some of this quality seems inborn, but it can be developed. It grows with confidence. Tell your players they must always want the ball. Part of the problem, where there is a problem, comes from lack of confidence. Some kids don't want the ball because they are afraid they will make a mistake. They somehow manage never to be open for a pass. Deal with this through practice. As skills improve, so does confidence. If a kid plays one-on-one (a great way for parents to get some exercise!), he will learn what he can do with the ball. He will learn that he can handle the ball, and he will want the ball more often.

FIGURE 4-6
MOVE TO THE BALL

The most important action in receiving a pass is to move or step to the ball; to reach out to receive it.

Move to the Ball

Unless the pass is part of a play, the receiver must reach for and, if possible, step to the ball. Defenders will look to steal the pass, so it's important to beat them to it. Many, many passes are stolen because the receiver was stationary, waiting for the ball. Teach your players to step to it, reach out their hands to receive it! Teach them to claim the ball! (See Figure 4-6.)

Give a Target

It's much easier on the passer if the receiver puts up a hand, palms out, to the spot she wants the ball. For instance, if a defender is on the right side, she should put up a left hand as the target.

Hands Must Be Soft

A basketball is big and very bouncy, so it's rather difficult to catch. Many kids tense up when the ball approaches, and this increases the chance that the ball will bounce off their hands.

Soft hands is a term used in many sports, including baseball and football. (In soccer, the term is soft feet.) Tell your player she must try to relax.

Shake the hands, loosen them up. Make them less rigid and tense. Practice passing and receiving and discuss this concept. Tell her to notice her hands, to make them soft, and then to notice the difference.

Keep the Eyes on the Ball

This is the key to catching anything in any sport. The ball is pretty big, and easy to see, but that does not lessen the need to concentrate on it. Watch the ball from the moment it leaves the passer's hands until it's in your hands. Maintain concentration. It's OK to *divide* concentration, to begin to *sense* what to do with the ball, but never take the eyes from it. The transition from the catch to the next movement, whether it is a dribble, pass or shot, requires control of the ball. Control begins with a solid reception.

PASSING DRILLS

We already discussed the best passing drill there is: A parent and a child or two children can just go out and have a catch. You don't need a basket, and this can be done anywhere. I used to do it all the time with my sons (just clear away breakables!). Passing off a concrete wall is useful for someone who is practicing alone.

Stress the Techniques

Talk about the importance of passing as you have a catch. Talk about the techniques, finger positions, rotation and stepping to the target. Talk about dynamics. Talk about receiving with soft hands, keeping the eye on the ball, moving to the ball and keeping body weight forward.

Tip Tap—A good drill for softening hands is to tip it back and forth between two players. I used to stand about 5 feet from my son and we would pass the ball quickly back and forth, as quickly as we could, almost *tipping* it back and forth. This drill forces the child to concentrate on the ball, and develops quicker reflexes.

Monkey-in-the-Middle—This is a good drill because it teaches dribbling, passing and receiving under pressure. Six players circle the key, a step or so back, with the "monkey" standing in the center of the key. Players can pass to anyone in the circle except the player next to them. They may dribble with the ball, but can't move more than a few feet to the right or left. The "monkey" tries to intercept or force a turnover. Whoever makes a mistake (five-seconds delay, bad pass, a missed reception, traveling) is the new monkey. Make sure the kids use the pivot move a lot. Watch the fouls; don't let the monkey reach in and foul.

Pass Away—This drill is like monkey-in-the-middle, but here it's two-on-two. Set up, using cones or towels, an area 20′ × 20′. No dribbling is allowed. The player with the ball may pivot but has only three seconds to pass. The defender counts the seconds out loud by thousands. The receiver must fake and feint to get free. Adjust the area size and timing to fit your players' age group. Younger players need less space.

On the Run—Two players start at one end of the court, or on their sidewalk or driveway, and run to the other end, passing back and forth. No dribbling is allowed. Watch for traveling fouls: Only one step is allowed before the ball must be passed.

Weaving—Three players run the length of the court in a weaving pattern as depicted in Figure 4-7. The weave is designed so that the ball stays in the center lane of the court. The player with the ball, having received it in the center lane, always passes to another player who is entering the center lane. The passer then runs to the side of the court vacated by the receiver. The receiver then does the same routine with the player on the other side of the court, and so on.

Medicine Man—Medicine balls are not used much these days, but they are great passing aides. Position players in two lines 5 to 10 feet apart and have them chest pass and two-hand overhead pass medicine balls back and forth to build passing strength.

Two-Quick

Two players stand 10 to 12 feet apart, each holding a ball. They pass rapidly to each other, one with a chest pass, one with a bounce pass. After a while they switch pass types.

Finger Tip Drill

For this simple reflex drill, hold the ball between the hands and slowly pass it from hand to hand. Gradually increase speed to the maximum, still tipping the ball back and forth. See how wide apart the hands can get at higher speeds.

FIGURE 4-7

THE WEAVE DRILL

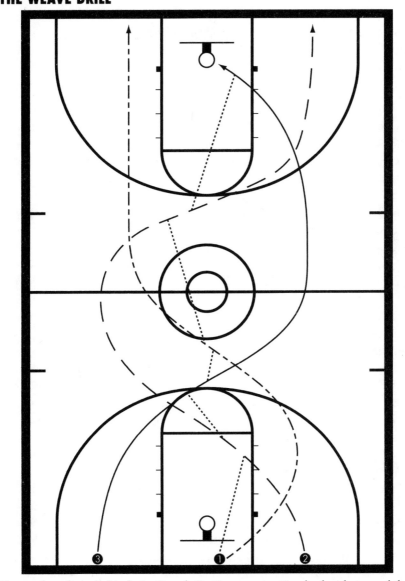

Players form lines behind #1, #2 and #3. #1 passes to #2, who heads toward the middle lane, and then #1 (weaves) runs upcourt into the right lane. #2 quickly passes to #3, who has curved toward the center lane, and then #2 weaves behind #3 and continues up the left lane. #3 passes to #1 who has returned to the center lane near mid-court. #1 passes to #2 who comes toward the middle lane from the left lane, and so on until the last player with the ball shoots a lay up.

Chapter Five

OFFENSE

As a coach or a parent, you must develop your players' feel for the game by discussing offensive concepts. To begin, select a set of play patterns for your team; although different coaches will employ different plays, the basic offensive concepts are the same everywhere. In this chapter, we will discuss these concepts and review some specific offensive plays. You and your players should review them together. Most kids don't know anything but pass and shoot, and an early understanding of concepts will go a long way in getting a kid some extra playing time and that oh-so-necessary experience.

Basketball is somewhere between football and soccer in play-making. Football has very specific plays that all players follow, while soccer has fewer plays, and the game flows more according to a set of concepts and the opportunities of the moment. Basketball more equally blends both plays and concepts. For instance, one *concept* is that players can free up a teammate to shoot by screening away his defender. The *play* is the specific plan designed to set up that screen. There are obviously several different ways to do it, and you could use several different players for the screen, but the concept is always the same. Kids need to understand concepts, and if they do they can often tailor their own plays to the immediate situation. Also, understanding concepts helps them understand what you as their coach are trying to do.

OFFENSIVE ZONES

When a team has the ball, the half-court area near their target basket becomes the offensive area of the court. It can be divided into five zones— the low post, high post, point, wing and corner. The plays discussed later in this chapter will focus upon these five zones. Generally the *post* positions are used to bring the ball underneath the basket for a shot while the *wing* and *corner* launch attacks from the outside. The point, wing and corner zones are also together referred to as the *perimeter.* Take a second look at Figure 1-5 in chapter one. Within these zones are critical areas established by different lines. The rectangular area under the basket, between the free throw lines, is called the lane or the paint. It is also called the three-second zone. There are small squares on either side of the free throw lines under the hoop called the blocks. Two more lines, called free throw stripes, are painted at intervals of 3 feet. The free throw or foul line is the diameter of a circle which, with the foul lane, is called the key (it looks sort of like a keyhole). The end of the court is called the baseline, and the mid-line of the court is also called the backcourt line. Offensive zones are often assigned numbers by the coach. Different coaches may have different terms; if so, your players will need to learn them. Language varies across the country.

OFFENSIVE CONCEPTS

The objective of offense is to move your players around the court in such a way that one of them is able to take a high percentage shot. If you have a dominant big player, get the ball to her under the basket. If you have a great outside shooter, run plays that will free her from her defender for a shot. If you have a great passer, use that ability with plays appropriately suited for quick passes. You must assess your team's strengths and employ plays that maximize those strengths. If you know your strengths and also understand how the following basic offensive concepts can utilize them, you can employ the plays that will give your team its best chance to win.

Take the High Percentage Shot

You've got to put the ball in the hoop! The bottom line of basketball is the team with the most points wins! Although we could debate (and we will later) about how important it is to win, I would certainly argue that sportsmanship must balance with competitiveness as the goal of youth athletics. It gripes me to see grammar school coaches playing the same kids all the time, sacrificing the development and confidence of the substitutes for a winning score. Nevertheless, the players who put the most points on the board will always see the most action. Good scorers are rare: They can't be kept on the bench!

There are many aspects of scoring. Offense grows out of defense, so scoring starts with a defensive rebound or a steal. It includes being able to control the ball through good passing while bringing it up the floor. But, in the final analysis, scoring comes from good shooting and good shooting comes from good shot selection.

This means that you need kids who can shoot, but more importantly, it means that you have to get them into a position for a *high percentage shot*, a shot as close to the hoop as possible and relatively free of defensive pressure. The way to get the open shot is a combination of speed, screening, faking, quickness and a lot of motion.

Each coach has his or her own system, a series of offensive plays within the context of an overall offensive strategy. The best strategy is usually to try to get the ball safely into the hands of the big guys underneath, or to pick off a defender so someone, usually one of the better shooters, has an open jump shot. The plays are designed to get all players moving in a pattern designed to break up, frustrate and confuse the defense. The ultimate goal is to free someone up for a high percentage shot.

Get It to the Post Man

The highest percentage shots are directly underneath, in the low post area. The bread-and-butter play of basketball is a pass to a big player underneath, posting up his defender or "flashing," cutting back and forth under the hoop from the free throw lines. If a team has a good, big center who knows how to post effectively and can make power moves underneath, that's about all they need. It's basketball heaven! In chapter one we discussed posting techniques. A bit later on, we will review the plays needed to get a good pass to the low post and to get the post man free underneath. The *concept* is to get the ball safely passed to a post player. (See Figure 5-1.)

Attack From the Wing

The real attack does not start from the point. The point is like a hinge on a door, feeding the ball to the wing. The point is usually too far from the low post to get a good pass into that area. Likewise, the corner is not the optimal place to start our attack since a player can easily get trapped there. The wing area is the quarterback zone for the actual attack. The great majority of passes from the point are to the wing area, and that's where the real action starts. The wing man, usually an off guard or shooting forward, can either make an individual move, shoot or drive; or she can pass to the post, to the corner, or back out to the point. (See Figure 5-2.)

The Pick

The workhorse offensive play is the *pick* or *screen*. These terms are pretty much used interchangeably anymore, although traditionally it's called a "pick" if the player to be freed has the ball, and a "screen" if the idea is to free up someone else to get the ball.

The screening technique is fairly simple. A player runs up to the side of the defender to be picked, preferably from a bit behind so she doesn't see him coming. Timing is important. If the offensive player approaches too early, the defender will have time to avoid him; too late, and a foul is possible from running into the defender.

FIGURE 5-1
THE LOW-POST ATTACK

This is a bread-and-butter concept of basketball. Get the ball in to a good, big player, clear everybody else out, and let her take the ball to the hoop.

Once there, the player spreads his legs wide, holds his elbows held out, and pulls his hands in close to his chest to avoid a foul. Have your player brace himself because the defender is likely to bang into him, and referees will rarely call a foul, unless it's flagrant. (See Figure 5-3.)

I play a lot of small three-on-three games near my home, and I *always* look to pick the defender from the player with the ball. It's second nature. It either frees the player to dribble or shoot, or it sets up a pick and roll (see below). I'm always amazed to see guys who never pick a defender. They stand around looking, and it never occurs to them to get involved because they never learned the concept. The pick is one of the two or three most basic offensive moves.

The Pick and Roll

The pick and roll is another bread-and-butter move, and your players must learn to appreciate its value. The pick and roll is based upon the pick concept and means that as soon as your player picks a defender, he pivots or rolls in the same direction his freed-up teammate is moving and moves

FIGURE 5-2
THE ATTACK FROM THE WING

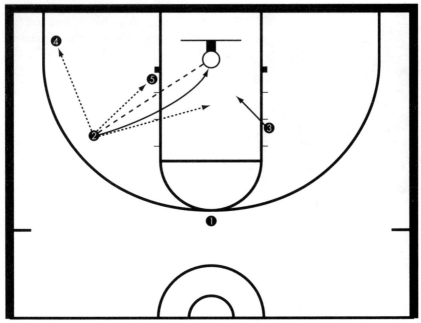

During this play, the wing (#2) passes to the corner (#4), the post (#5) or to the other wing (#3), as the latter player cuts into the lane. The wing can also shoot or drive to the hoop.

parallel to him, with hand up, expecting a pass. Usually, the picked defender is now out of the play so there is a two-on-one situation with the remaining picker. Often, the picker becomes free, since his defender now switches to cover the dribbler. If so, then the picker rolls toward the basket for an easy pass and shot. (See Figure 5-4.)

Often, one player on offensive can play at the high post in a stationary position while a guard dribbles close to her. The high-post player picks the dribbler's defender. If the pick is successful in freeing the ball handler, then the picker can roll behind the dribbler. In this case, the picker becomes a trailer and can get a rebound.

Give and Go

The Give and Go is the *best move in basketball*. It doesn't involve a screen, just pure speed. A player simply passes to a teammate, and as he passes, he explodes forward, past his defender, and looks for a quick return pass. If done right, it often leads to an easy lay-up. The give and go works very

FIGURE 5-3
THE PICK

Step 1. This play, also called the screen, frees up a closely guarded teammate to dribble or shoot, or sets up the pick and roll. Here the screen is set up by the offensive player on the right.

Step 2. In this successful pick, the defender is blocked from pursuing the dribbler who now penetrates closer to the hoop.

well at young ages. It goes without saying that the player must also act as the middleman on a give and go, receiving the pass and giving it back quickly. (See Figure 5-5.)

Don't Be Too Quick to Dribble

Kids develop a bad habit of dribbling too quickly after receiving a pass. However, once you begin dribbling, you forgo other options. Encourage your players to take the time to look inside toward the hoop for an opportunity. Obviously, if there is an opening or some space in front of the dribbler, he should advance the ball. But, if your player is guarded, he shouldn't dribble, or "put the ball down," too quickly. Dribbling is only one of the initial opportunities. The best players look for the opportunities even before they get the ball.

Pass to an Open Space

We covered this in chapter four, but it's such an important offensive concept that it bears repeating here. Open space is any space around a receiver in which a pass can be made safely. It's most desirable to pass to space in the direction the receiver is heading; however, if he is guarded that space may be very small. To assure the opponent doesn't get the pass, make it snappy,

FIGURE 5-4
THE PICK AND ROLL

Step 1. If during a pick play (see the *pick* photos on page 71), the defenders switch positions to pick up the dribbler, the offensive player who initiated the pick must react and begin to roll, that is, turns, in a counterclockwise spin to face the ball handler.

Step 2. The roll opens the offensive receiver up for a pass and the chance for an easy lay-up.

use fakes and don't broadcast it. A pass directly to a player may freeze his action or lead to a fumble, and certainly slows overall momentum.

Individual Moves for Getting Open

Basketball is a team sport first and foremost. Championships are rarely won with just one good player. Every player must be able to do things on his own. Coaches look at *numbers*: points, rebounds, steals, assists, turnovers. The kids with numbers are going to play more. A lot of kids hardly ever get their hands on the ball, and then quickly get rid of it, passing it off as if they don't even want it. Be patient with these kids: most go through this at some point. Only a few kids are stars. However, by learning a few individual moves, in time the player within will blossom. I firmly believe that most kids

FIGURE 5-5

THE GIVE AND GO

Step 1. This is the *best* move in basketball because it relies only on speed, and, if done right, results in an easy lay-up. First, the point guard passes the ball to a pivot player, who is only a relay for the getting the ball back to the point guard.

Step 2. The point guard fakes right, then cuts left toward the hoop.

Step 3. The pivot player returns the ball to the point guard, who drives to the hoop for the lay-up.

have athletes inside them, and they can all improve. It just takes some desire, some faith, some encouragement and a few ideas.

Explain to your players that they won't get the ball passed to them if defenders are closely guarding them. They have to find a way to get open. There are two good ways to do that, individually, without the help of another teammate's screen: the jab step and the circle.

Jab Step

To execute a jab step the player steps toward the defender and then suddenly and quickly stops and comes back to her original position. The defender will tend to back up a bit at first, which gets her weight going backward, off balance. Usually, the jab step will get a player open for a good second or so. It's enough.

The Circle

Another method for evading a defender is the circle. Just revolve around the defender for a half or full circle. This confuses him, gets him off balance, and the player can then quickly dart out for a pass before the defender recovers.

Timing

Timing is always important. A player needs to sense when a teammate will look her way to pass, and try to get open at that time. Timing will come with experience.

The Value of Motion

Another way to get open, and a key to offensive play, is simply to get on the move. With motion, a player will get open at some point. Players need to cut into the lanes, flash from one side of the lane to another, or sneak behind the hoop, along the baseline, and come in through the back door. The back door concept is based on the fact that defensive players are usually looking up court, and may not see someone slipping in from behind. The worst thing to do is just stand around!

Move Off the Ball

Many skills are hard to achieve, but the easiest of all is one of the most important: hustling. Hustle is key to basketball, and moving, even without the basketball, is what makes teams winners. It's the *movement off the ball* that creates possibilities for successful *action on the ball*. With or without the ball, a player should think about where to go. Her play pattern will give her a direction; but she must then choose how *best* to get there.

It's hard to catch a pass when closely guarded, so she must constantly

FIGURE 5-6

JUMP STOP

The *jump stop*—jumping to the ball and landing on both feet—puts a player in the position of pivoting on either foot in preparation for receiving a pass.

think about how to shed her opponent: If the job is to screen, where is the best spot to set it up and what is the right timing? What is the ball handler seeing? What is she thinking about? If the play breaks down, what do I need to do? Screen? Shed the defender? Screen someone else to free a teammate up for a pass?

Tell players they are always in the game, and always impacting the team, every second, for the good or for the bad.

Moving to Get a Pass

Getting open is just the first step. Players must then catch the pass. We discussed in chapter four the need to move to the ball and reach out with the hands for the pass. This will avoid many steals. Remind your players to always anticipate the pass.

When moving to get a pass, a player should *jump-stop*. This means that he simply jumps to the ball and lands on both feet. From this position, he can pivot on either foot. If the feet touch the ground unevenly, only the first foot to touch can be the pivot. (See Figure 5-6.)

Taking the Shot

When an open player catches a pass within her shooting range, especially within 12 feet of the hoop, the first thought must be to shoot. That's the name of the game: High percentage shots must be taken quickly. Even a poor shooter has a good chance to sink a short jumper. She shouldn't hesitate! She shouldn't think! She must shoot very quickly before a defender comes on. At that range there's not much time, only a fraction of a second. How often have you heard the fans groan when an unsure kid fails to take a short jump shot? Players must learn to think about scoring.

Following the Shot

Once the shot is off, unless you instruct that player to stay back to stop a fast break by the defense, the shooter must follow the shot. About one in six rebounds will bound back toward the shooter, and a good follow-up move will get many of them. Offensive rebounds are usually those that bounce out a good distance, since defensive players usually have the best position for short rebounds.

That's the ticket. Get open, catch the pass, fake, drive, shoot and rebound. Make the moves, make it happen. Challenge your players! Drill them to do these things.

OFFENSIVE PLAY PATTERNS

Now we combine the concepts and the individual moves into a play. Actually, every single movement in a basketball game can be called a play. Give and go, screen, pick and roll, jab, flash, baseline drive—these are all plays. The best players make their own plays, within the structure of the team's overall offensive motion. The best plays are not necessarily the ones called by the coach or signaled by the point guard as he dribbles down court. The best plays are those that seize the opportunity of the moment: a defender off balance or out of position, a height mismatch, an open lane.

However, it's important that the overall movement of the offensive players be orderly and consistent. You want to keep your players moving. Young players often get mesmerized by the action and tend to stand around and watch their teammates. It's helpful to the passer to know ahead of time where her teammates are going to be. These plays are called *patterns*, or continuous motion offenses.

Patterns are often a series of plays designed to set players in motion using screens or speed to get someone open for the high percentage shot. If no player is open, the play continues to move players around until someone is free, or until someone makes it happen. At any time, a player may seize an opportunity. All players, while running the pattern, should look for an opportunity to score or hit an open player.

These play patterns are usually very simple. A young team employs only one or two such patterns. Every coach should have at least one in mind.

The Shuffle

The shuffle is probably one of the most widely used play patterns in basketball. I learned it as a kid, and I've seen it used many times since. In this pattern, the players set up and move to the positions shown in Figure 5-7 as the point guard (#1) reaches the top of the key. The off guard (#2) shuffle cuts, that is, runs into and across the lane, cutting close to any nearby defender for a screen from a forward (#3) positioned at the high post. In the first diagram, the point guard looks to pass to the cutting off guard who then drives to the basket or dishes the ball off to one of the big players underneath (#4 and #5).

In the second diagram, #1 can't get the ball to #2, so he looks for #4, who then flashes across the lane behind #2.

If that doesn't work, then as the third diagram shows, #1 uses #3 as a screen and dribbles into the lane, or dishes it off to #3.

If after all this nothing looks good, #1 just passes off to #5, who comes out to the wing, #3 heads to the point, and #1 then heads to the low post spot originally held by #4. Note that the pass to #5 in the wing is a good give and go opportunity for #1.

If nothing worked, then the ball is passed by #5 back to #3 at the point and the play is run again from the opposite side. By then, the players are in place for another shuffle.

The players must all know how to move from position to position. It seems like a lot to know, but that's what practice is for. The point is that, during the shuffle, all players are in constant motion all over the floor, creating opportunities. Usually the pattern needs to be run only once or twice before an opportunity is created or before a player tries to make something happen. The shuffle is called a *continuity pattern* because if it fails, the team is already set up to run it the other way.

The Scissor

Also known as a single-pivot, the scissor is another common play, although it's not a continuous pattern. Two guards (#1 and #2) bring the ball up court and, as they approach the key, the center (#3) moves to the high post. He receives the ball, and the guards crisscross in a scissor move in front of him. The center may give the ball to either guard as they pass

FIGURE 5-7

THE SHUFFLE

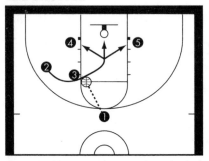

First shuffle: #2 cuts around the high post #3 and drives to shoot or to dish off to #4 or #5. Note an option I like here is for #5 to circle #4 backdoor and return to his spot just after #2 drives. This moves clear the right side for #2.

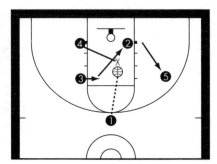

Second shuffle: If #2 didn't get the pass (not open for a pass), then #4 immediately cuts behind him looking for a pass. If you used the option, then #4 follows #5 across the lane. If no pass to #4 is open then #3 starts to float across to the pivot spot in the middle of the key and #5 drifts to the wing.

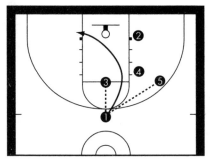

Third shuffle: Since #1 could not get the ball to either #2 or #4, he cuts around #3's screen to drive to the hoop. If he can't get through he passes back out to #5 or #3.

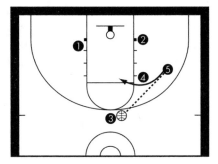

Reshuffle: If nothing was open anywhere, then the players are positioned for another shuffle the other way. #5 passes back to #3, and a reverse shuffle begins with #5 cutting around #4's screen, and so forth.

in front of him. If not, he turns to face the hoop and may either look again to pass to a guard, or dribble and shoot himself. The forwards (#4 and #5) can also post-interchange underneath, creating another passing opportunity. (Post-interchange is described below.) The point guard circles and returns to the point for a pass back out if the play fails. (See Figure 5-8.)

A variation of the scissor is to have #4 stay at the low post and #5 circle

FIGURE 5-8

THE SCISSOR

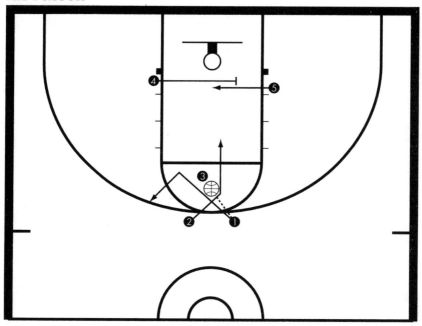

#1 passes to #3 at the high post pivot. #2 quickly cuts by #3 for a hand off, and #1 follows behind #2 but drops back if she doesn't get the ball. #3 can hand off to either guard, or turn to shoot or drive to the hoop. She can also pass to #5 whose defender is screened by #4. If nothing works, pass out to #1 for a new play.

back-door behind him and around to the high post. This clears out the whole right side for a guard (#2), and frees #5 for a pass.

Post-Interchange

We talked earlier about getting the ball to the wing and then trying to pass it to the big player posting up underneath. Another option is to have two big players (#4 and #5) line up on the opposite low post blocks and then switch positions. (See Figure 5-9.) The player moving away from the ball (#4) stops momentarily under the hoop to screen the oncoming defender of the other big player (#5) who is flashing across the lane toward the middle. The center (#5) is now free to receive a pass underneath and should, in the best case, get the ball just as she reaches the screen. The screening player is always closest to the baseline so the receiving player can get the pass.

FIGURE 5-9

POST INTERCHANGE

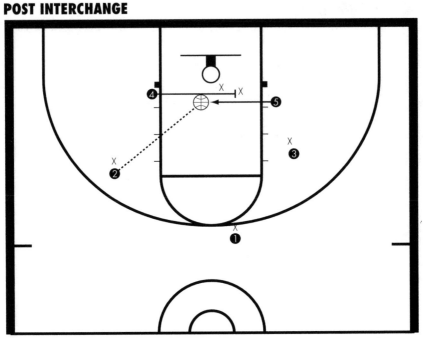

The big players underneath should always try to screen for each other. If #4 doesn't get a pass to his low post position, then he should turn and screen for #5 who cuts across the lane for a pass.

Outside Pick and Roll

A nice play I've seen in youth basketball has the point guard (#1) pass to a shooting forward (#3). (See Figure 5-10.) Then the point guard darts to the high post and picks the player defending the off guard (#2). The off guard cuts around the screen into the lane for the ball. She can either drive or dump off to the rolling point guard. The center (#5) clears her side by cutting back-door behind #4.

Offensive Patterns According to Defense Employed

The selection of offensive patterns will vary depending on the type of defense used by the opponent. In a *man-to-man* defense each defender is responsible for defending a specific player. Usually players defend opponents of similar size. In a *zone* defense, defenders are assigned to defend an area, and any opponent coming into their area is their responsibility. Of course, if no opponent comes into their area they must help out in any adjoining area with multiple opponents.

FIGURE 5-10

OUTSIDE PICK AND ROLL

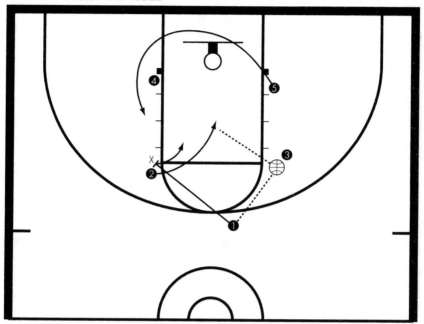

#1 passes to #3 and then proceeds to screen for #2. #5 cuts backdoor behind #4 to clear out the right side. #3 passes to #2 driving, or to #1 rolling off his screen, or to #5 at the high post.

Motion patterns such as the shuffle work best against man-to-man defenses. Other plays using screens, the give and go, pick and roll, and jab steps work better against man-to-man defense but may be used against zone defenses as well. However, it is tough to get inside against a zone, and so many of these movements are effective only out in the perimeter areas. As we will discuss later, the zone is sometimes banned in youth basketball so that the kids learn real defense. It's banned in the pros, too, in order to promote more action under the hoop. It's just not basketball. However, if it's to be used, it is easy for kids to learn because it's so simple.

A zone forces outside shooting because, essentially, defensive players bunch up around the lane. This defense allows defenders to front the big offensive players underneath and deny passes to them. It also makes it difficult for offensive players to drive into the congestion of defenders.

Cutting into the lane, into the gaps of the zone, is one way to split the zone. It requires a good hard passer to thread the needle with crisp passes. Post-interchange plays also work well against a zone. Offensive teams can

FIGURE 5-11

WHEEL PATTERN

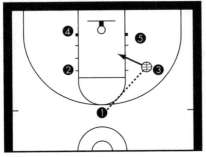

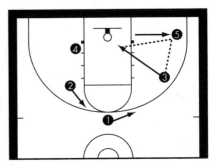

#1 passes to #3 who looks to shoot or drive.

If she can't make a move, #3 passes to the corner and looks for a give and go. As soon as #3 moves in, #2 and #1 begin to turn the wheel, floating to the right.

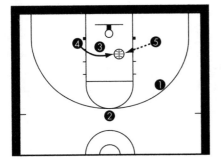

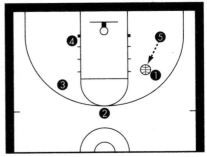

If #5 doesn't get the ball to #3, then #3 picks for #4 who flashes across the lane for a pass.

If nothing was open, then pass out to #1 to start over again working the wheel on the other side.

try to overload a zone to one side with two offensive players in an area guarded by only one defender. They can give each other screens to provide for short outside shots, pick and roll, or give and go plays.

The Wheel Pattern

A nice offense against a zone is a wheel-type motion. (See Figure 5-11.) It not only overloads the zone, but it keeps everyone in motion. The players line up in point (#1), two wings (#2 and #3) and two forwards (#4 and #5). There are four possible motions.

The first is a pass from point to #3 wing. The wing is free to drive or shoot.

If nothing is available, the second motion is wing to corner (#5). This can work as a give and go back to the wing who cuts to the hoop. The wing can also set up in a low post for a pass from the corner.

Otherwise, in the third motion, the wing screens for #4 who flashes across the lane.

Finally, the corner may hit #4, or give it back to #1, who has moved into the wing. Everyone revolves like a wheel—#2 goes to point, #3 goes to opposite wing, #4 returns to forward, and everyone is set up for the same or another play.

Give, Go and Wheel

A good beginner pattern, useful against any defense involves players in a series of possible *give and go* moves. Give and go plays work well from the point position using a wing, or from the wing using a corner player. If a give and go is not executed, then the players spin the wheel and try another. (See Figure 5-12.)

Fast Break

This offensive play starts after a defensive rebound. The rebounder (#5) turns and immediately passes to an outlet (#3) on the sideline. The key is for the guard to always be there. The guard on the side of the court with the ball action usually has the responsibility to head to the same spot on every rebound and be ready for the outlet pass.

As the ball is passed to the outlet, the point guard (#1) in the center lane and player closest to the far sideline (#2) head to the other two fast break lanes; one lane is down the middle and the other two on opposite sides of the court. The outlet (#3) breaks up court looking to pass quickly to his teammate in the center lane. The ball handler drives up mid-court and looks to pass to either of the sideline breakers as they move to the hoop. The original rebounder (#5) and the other player near the basket (#4) head toward the other end to help out, possibly rebounding after the fast break or defending in case the ball is turned over to the other team. This play requires speed, endurance, speed dribbling, and the ability to make a lay-up at full throttle.

Out-of-Bounds Play

Each team needs a few *out-of-bounds plays* for getting possession of the ball when defense is pressing. One is needed to inbound under the opponent's basket, one for mid-court and one for under your own basket. Figures 5-14A and 5-14B suggest two patterns which can be used for any

FIGURE 5-12
GIVE, GO AND WHEEL

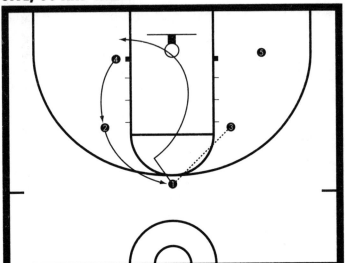

Point guard #1 passes to wing #3, then #1 V-cuts for a give and go toward the hoop. If #3 can't pass back to #1, #1 replaces #4, and #4 and #2 turn the wheel counterclockwise to reestablish the 1-2-2.

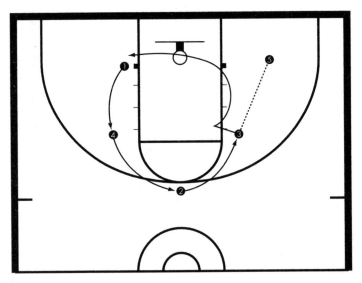

#3 still has the ball. She passes to #5, then v-cuts for a give and go. If #5 can't get her the ball, then the players again turn the wheel. #5 should make a move, such as passing to #2 for another give and go, or get the ball out to the top of the key for another play.

FIGURE 5-13

THREE-LANE FAST BREAK

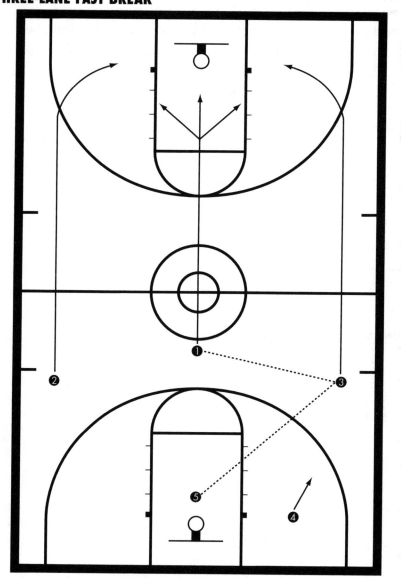

The classic fast break has the rebounder (#5) passing to outlet (#3) who in turn passes to midcourt (#1). #1 drives down the middle as the two wide players (#2 and #3) streak up the sideline. All three angle toward the hoop. The remaining two players, #4 and #5, trail the play.

FIGURE 5-14A

INBOUNDING UNDERNEATH

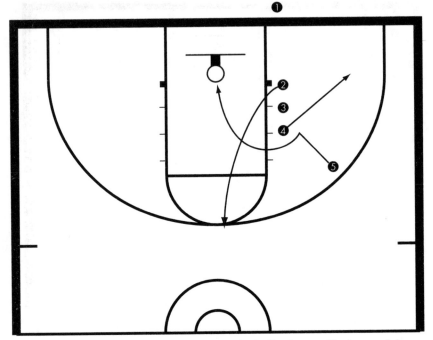

Under your own hoop inbound: As #1 taps the ball, #5 cuts off #4 toward the hoop, tapping #4's back. Upon feeling this tap #4 steps to the right for a pass. #2 rushes to the top of the key for a deep pass in case #4 and #5 are guarded. #1 passes or fakes to #5, then looks to #4 or to stationary #3. If nothing works, look to dump out to #2.

inbounds situation. The ones suggested work well for inbounding from sidecourt as well as for underneath.

Inbound and Break the Press

Sometimes defenders will closely guard the inbound pass after a basket is scored. This is called a *press,* or *full court press.* As noted earlier it is often prohibited in youth basketball.

Remember what I said earlier about the importance of dribbling? If you have a good ball handler, she can break a press just by dribbling around defenders. Inbound to her and get everyone else out of the way. If you need more help, get your biggest player with good hands and some dribbling ability to mid-court. Since there are only 10 seconds allowed to get the ball past the mid-court line, a big player can usually catch a high pass at mid-court if time is running out.

FIGURE 5-14B

INBOUNDING FROM THE SIDELINE

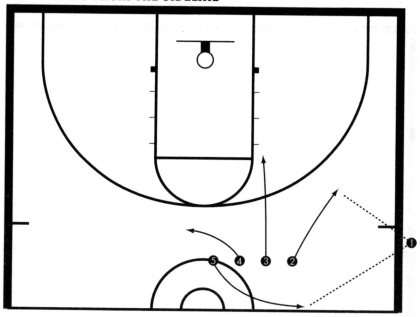

2 cuts toward the corner, #3 heads toward the lane, #4 heads away from the ball, and #5 moves toward the ball, backcourt if necessary. All defenders are spread out. #5 is primary receiver, #2 is next.

Figure 5-15 provides a good inbound play to break the press. The two best dribblers (#2 and #3) screen each other's defender hoping at least one of them gets free for the inbound. Whoever gets the ball heads up court. Meanwhile, a big player (#5) positions himself near mid-court to help if needed.

Center Tap Plays

A *center tap* occurs at the beginning of the game as well as any time officials disagree or when play is stopped for injury. Two players face each other at center court (at the beginning of the game) or at the center of the foul line closest to where play was stopped in other situations. The other players position themselves outside of the circle on the floor. The referee throws the ball straight up between the two players in the middle, and they each endeavor to tap the ball to a teammate.

If you are sure you can win the tap, then use the play in Figure 5-16A to tap directly to a guard (#2), and have him pass to one of two other players (#3 and #4) who immediately head towards the basket. If you are

FIGURE 5-15

INBOUND AND BREAK THE PRESS

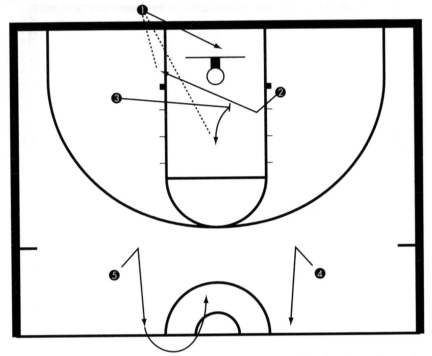

After opponent's basket with full court press defense: #1 has ball out of bounds. #4 and #5 fake toward the ball and then head up court to draw their men away; however #5, a big player, loops back to backcourt to help out if needed. #3 screens for #2 who fakes left and cuts to #1 for the ball. #1 can also pass to #3 who rolls off the screen up court. #1 gets open for a pass back if the receiver, #2 or #3 gets double covered. #5 is open for a high pass in an emergency.

unsure or expect to lose the tap, you can't afford to send players toward the offensive basket. Instead, send one immediately to the defensive basket, and the other players cover probable receivers. (See Figure 5-16B.)

OFFENSIVE DRILLS

Here are many drills and their variations that you can simplify, as needed, and compound as the players mature.

Walk-Throughs

Whatever play patterns you choose must be drilled until they are second nature. Hand out diagrams and talk the players through the moves. It's far easier for your players to understand a play if they see it first. Next, walk

FIGURE 5-16A

CENTER TAP PLAY

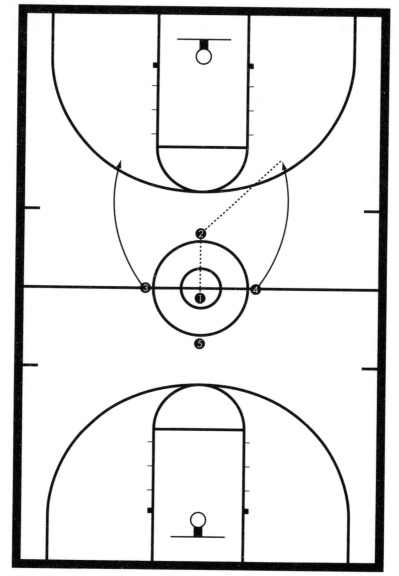

Sure you can win the tap: #1 taps forward to #2, #3 and #4 cut toward the basket for a quick pass from #2. #5 stays back to defend.

FIGURE 5-16B

CENTER TAP PLAY

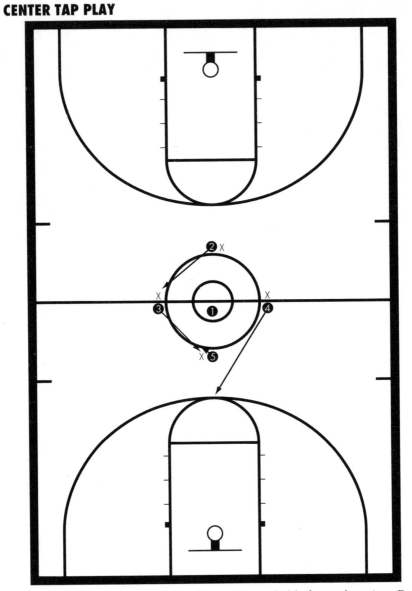

Sure you will lose the tap: #3 and #5 knife to the probable forward receiver, B. #4 heads toward defensive basket. #2 knifes toward X, the other probable receiver. Don't move till ball is thrown.

through the pattern several times, slowly adding light defense; then start running the pattern against full pressure. Note that a kid who may be a bit less skilled overall becomes more valuable if he can run the pattern well. Some kids are very coachable in this regard. Don't ignore the value of those who simply do what they are told.

Three-on-Two-on-One

One of the most popular drills for years, the Three-on-Two-on-One is fun, and is great for getting a team in shape. It practices a running fast break game, and incorporates shooting, defense, rebounding and speed dribbling. For young beginners, you may wish to start just with the three-on-two drill. After the three players make a basket or lose the ball, bring in five new players. For more experienced players, the drill can flow directly into the two-on-one. Whoever lost the ball, missed or made the shot among the three players must then defend against the two previous defenders while they drive down the court to try and score. While the two-on-one is in progress, two new defenders come on the floor and set up. Once the two-on-one is completed by a rebound or score, those three same players start the fast break again against the two new defenders. (See Figure 5-17.) The drill I offer is a continuous drill, and is much better when learned by the team.

Crisscross

I include two crisscross drills here: a simple crisscross off a pivot man, and a screen, crisscross and roll. After the players know the pattern, you may add some defenders. (See Figure 5-18.)

Stop, Pivot, Go

Footwork drills are essential. This one is a favorite of mine because the pivot and spin are fundamental foot skills which greatly expand a player's ability to navigate the floor through defensive traffic. The *stop, pivot, go* drill allows players to practice footwork without pressure. By running directly at a defender, we get her to lean back a bit. The jump-stop and spin movement depicted in Figure 5-19 allows the offensive player to present a clear target for a pass by spinning to face the passer.

Reverse Cuts

These are also excellent footwork drills. Players learn to fake and feint, and dash past defenders for easy lay-ups. With good footwork, the move is made easier. (See Figure 5-20.)

FIGURE 5-17

THREE-ON-TWO-ON-ONE DRILL

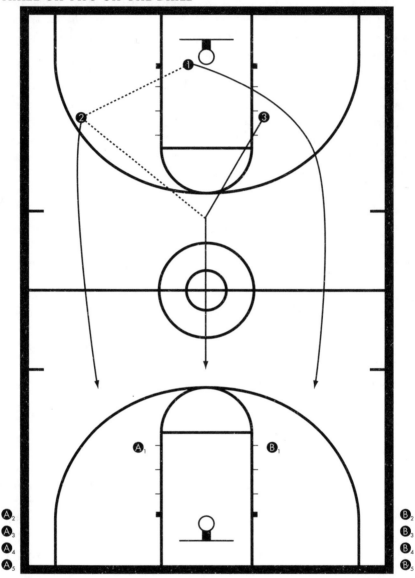

#1 stands under the hoop and banks the ball off the board to simulate a rebound. She yells "Ball!" when she gets the rebound and passes it to outlet #2. #3 runs to midcourt to get the ball from #2, and #1 and #2 head down the sideline. They try to score against defenders A and B. Beginners can stop here and bring on a new crew. Otherwise, after a rebound, steal, lost ball or score, A or B grabs the ball and, without *inbounding*, immediately head the other way to score.

FIGURE 5-18
CRISSCROSS DRILL

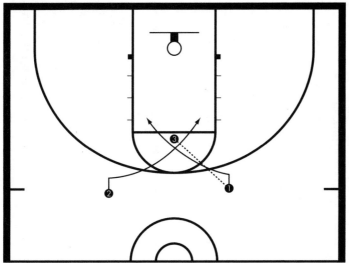

#1 passes to the pivot #3 and cuts off his left hip. #2 follows faking right and then cutting off #3's right hip. #3 hands off to either guard to turns to shoot or drive.

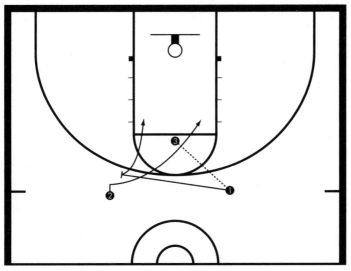

Roll variation: #1 passes to #3 and then screens #2's man. #2 fakes left then cuts off #3's right hip. #1 rolls clockwise, pivotting off right foot. #3 can pass to either guard, or turn to drive or shoot.

FIGURE 5-19

STOP, PIVOT AND GO DRILL

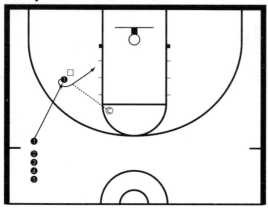

Place a chair or dummy defender at the wing area. Players line up along the sideline. First player runs at the chair, jump stops, then pivots off the inside foot counterclockwise (from the left side of the court) facing the coach or a guard in the key who then passes the ball for a lay-up. Do this from both sides. You can form two lines to run it alternatively from each side.

FIGURE 5-20

REVERSE CUT DRILLS

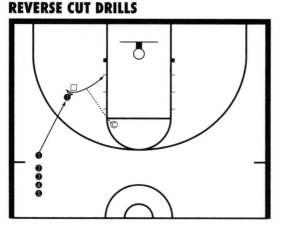

Place a chair or dummy defender at the wing. Players line up. First player runs at chair, jump stops, makes a fake to the right, pushes off with the right for a short step to the left, and then takes a large step with the right driving past the defender, stretching for a pass. The coach or guard in the key passes the ball for a lay-up. A variation to cut inside the defender is to fake right, then transfer weight to left foot for a long right step followed by a long left step by the defender, again stretching forward for the pass.

Chapter Six

DEFENSE

The images most associated with basketball are those of Michael Jordan twisting high in the air for a reverse slam dunk, or Larry Bird popping in a three-pointer. However, more and more, we herald the quickness of the diminutive Spud Webb stealing a pass or a Shaquille O'Neal rejecting an attempted shot.

It's called defense, and you need to talk regularly to your players about its importance. Kids often play poorly on defense: They fail to stay between their opponent and the hoop, allow players to drive around them, are easily faked out and miss opportunities to steal the ball by not being alert. These are the four primary weaknesses of kids defensively, so make sure your players understand them. Parents can help by reiterating the idea at home.

DEFENSE IS A STATE OF MIND

Anyone can be a good defensive player. It's much easier to do things without the ball than with it: The ball slows a player down. Defense is mainly a matter of desire, hustle, agility, energy and endurance. Sure, there are skills, and we'll discuss them, but defense is more a state of mind: It's playing as though the opponent has no right to the ball whatsoever.

A good defensive team seems frantic to get the ball back. A good defensive player always knows where the ball is and always looks for a chance to get her hands on it. Defense *wants* the ball.

As a coach, you can talk about this concept, repeatedly. If a player gets the message and becomes ball-crazy on the floor, it could be the beginning of an excellent ball player. The amount of playing time a kid gets is usually closely associated with her all-around ability to contribute. Coaches know they will have only a couple players who can score, and need players who can do other things.

A poor defensive player is a liability to the team. A coach can give playing time to poor offensive players—they can be hidden better. But nothing upsets coaches more than poor defensive effort. Such players will face a lot of bench time.

DEFENSIVE CONCEPTS

There are a number of defensive concepts which need to be impressed upon young players. Remember, defense is mainly attitude, and if your player gets that idea, it will help him immeasurably.

Transition Play: Get Back and Set Up

You can't play defense on the wrong end of the court. Players must get back to their defensive post or assignment very quickly when the other team gets the ball. It's one thing to see a tired player come up court slowly on offense. It's entirely another to react slowly on defense. Players who do will soon find the bench. Getting back on defense is a time to sprint. Many games are lost in this transitional part of the game.

Catch the Dribbler, Pivot and Defend

When a player is beaten by a ball handler, he must turn and run down-court, try to get in front of the ball handler, and set up to defend again. Remember, a defender can almost always outrun a dribbler. The common error is going directly for the ball, reaching or bumping the dribbler, often resulting in a foul. Get back and set up. Catch the player first, then pivot and defend.

Stay Low and Apply Great Pressure

This is the heart of a good defense, upsetting the player with the ball in every possible way. Flailing arms, shaking hand movements, grunts, groans, anything that works to distract the opponent. As long as your players don't foul!

A player doesn't need the ball to fake: A defensive player can and should fake body movements pretending to charge the ball handler to get him to commit himself to a move. It all serves to confuse the opposition. I've even heard some players talk to the man they are guarding, to get him riled up, to get him thinking too much about what he is doing. I don't encourage this: It seems unsportsmanlike. But players should be encouraged to talk with their bodies, and the message to be sent is pure disruption. (See Figure 6-1.)

The big idea in defensive play is to stay low in the triple-threat position. The low position allows your players to stay fairly close, about a step or arm's length away, and apply great pressure. Think pressure!

FIGURE 6-1
PRESSURE

Defense is about intimidation through physical presence and through pressure from a low and stable triple-threat defensive stance.

Keep the Action Wide, Away From the Lane

This just makes common sense. The free throw lane area—the low and high posts—is where high percentage shots are taken. We want to always deny this inside route to the dribbler or passer. Force the play to stay wide, along the sideline.

The lowest percentage shots are those taken from the corners. These shots are long, and there is no backboard to afford perspective or to allow a lucky bank to an errant shot. Your players should force the ball into the corner if at all possible. Also, the corners act as a natural trap to a player, eliminating options and allowing the defense to bottle up and really frustrate a player. On a baseline drive, you must protect the line and force the ball back out into traffic, where other defenders can help. A successful baseline drive yields a very high percentage offensive shot.

Avoid Bad Fouls

There *are* times to foul: stopping an otherwise easy lay-up, trying to regain possession in the final minutes of the game, fouling a player who is a terrible foul shooter. Also, there are good fouls, particularly when the defense has not accumulated many fouls and the player thinks he can take the ball away from a mediocre ball handler. So he reaches in and risks the referee's call.

However, when the defense has accumulated five fouls, the other team shoots a one-and-one foul shot. At that point, usually late in the game, fouls can become very costly. Also, once a player personally accumulates five fouls, he is ejected from the game. The big players accumulate the most fouls since there is so much action underneath the hoop. Young kids tend to get sloppy, and can accumulate fouls rapidly.

Stick 'Em Up—It's very easy to make body contact underneath. Any movement of the defensive player when attempting to block a shot will usually result in a foul call. Many youth referees will blow the whistle automatically on attempts to block a shot if the players' bodies are close. The best recourse when defending a chippie or short jump shot under the hoop, where bodies are always touching, is just to stand still and erect, hands straight up. (See Figure 6-2.) I call it "stick 'em up!" It gives up the two points, but puts some pressure on the shot. It can also draw an offensive foul. At the very least, it saves our big player from foul trouble.

Deny the Ball—When an opposing player is underneath, you want to deny her the ball, that is, prevent her receiving a pass. Denying players is the cornerstone of defensive strategy today. Most teams use it. If a player, especially a big player, is in a low post close to the hoop, she will nearly always score if she gets the ball. Make sure she doesn't get it by *fronting* her, that is, playing between her and the ball, or at least playing to the inside of her and getting an arm around her into the passing lane. This generally works only close to the hoop, within 6 feet of it.

If fronting is done farther away, the alley oop pass over the defender is a very effective way to break it. Use fronting only when a player is flashing under the hoop or in a low post. In a zone defense, there is usually another defensive player nearby who can defend if the alley oop gets to the post man. When denying the ball from the high post, keep the hand in the passing lane. (See Figure 6-3.)

Defending Against a Pick—*Switching* is a tricky defensive concept to apply, but an effective defense to a pick or screen. When an offensive screen or pick successfully frees a ball handler from her defender, a new defender needs to cover the ball handler. The defender who was guarding the offensive screener is the one who must usually switch to cover the

FIGURE 6-2

DEFENSE UNDERNEATH

Almost any movement underneath will result in a foul. A defending player should just stand erect with her hands straight up.

free player. However, this defender must not switch too quickly, thereby abandoning the screener she was guarding; so she *shows* herself to the dribbler instead, feigning that she is going to guard the dribbler, causing the dribbler to slow down a bit and thus buying time for more defensive assistance to arrive.

Nevertheless, when a switch occurs, it's often just what the offense wanted. The screener is momentarily left alone and can usually *roll* into the lane in preparation for a pass. So the defender who switched needs to hedge the bet a bit by showing herself to the ball handler while still keeping an eye on the player she left alone. The defender who was screened must drop back quickly to help out.

FIGURE 6-3
DENY THE PASS

The passing lane underneath the hoop must be denied the offense by extending the arm into the lane, or, better, by fronting with the whole body.

Farther from the hoop, a defender should discourage a pass using her extended hand, but should stay slightly behind the receiver to prevent an alley-oop pass over the head.

We have discussed this already, but it bears repeating here: *The best way to defend a pick is to fight through it*. Usually other defensive teammates will see the pick as it is being formed and alert the player to be screened so she can *step through it*, that is, step gingerly between the screener and the dribbler or *sink behind it*, that is, step behind the screener. The best course is usually to sink back to avoid fouling the screener. The defender who was covering the screener should also step back to let the defender covering the dribbler through, and also be prepared to switch quickly if needed. Note that when a screened defensive player sinks behind the screener, she can easily cover the screener on a switch. If a switch is to occur, the free defender must call it out loud. This alerts the screened defender to guard the screener. Otherwise, when fighting through a pick, the defender should get the leg in front of the screener and squirm through her and the ball carrier without fouling.

As noted, however, the key to defending against a screen is for the defender who was guarding the screener to *show himself* to the ball handler, thus applying some pressure, while keeping a close eye on the

FIGURE 6-4
DEFEND THE PICK

To defend against the pick, the defender (in the dark T-shirt, left) tries to step through the pick as her teammate begins to "show" herself to the dribbler.

screener to see if she rolls to the hoop. Sink back and watch both offensive players, slow them down until help arrives. (See Figure 6-4.)

The Trap

The trap is a great defensive weapon. It involves two defenders surrounding a dribbler as soon as she stops dribbling, particularly when near a sideline and definitely when in any one of the four corners. When the dribbler is in the corner, the second defender comes in right away, particularly if the dribbler looks as though she can't get a pass off immediately. Of course, if the player is in the act of or preparing to pass, the trap is off. This play is usually used against a short player or one who is not a good ball handler. A well-executed trap will often force an errant pass, result in a steal, or, if the ball handler can't execute a pass in five seconds, the defense is awarded the ball. (See Figure 6-5.)

DEFENSE STANCE

The most important fundamental in most sports is proper form. It is the foundation upon which a player uses his individual ability. Good form will best position a player to execute a move. It maximizes quickness, the ability to react and the balance needed to launch a good shot. A proper

FIGURE 6-5
THE TRAP

Anytime two defenders can trap a dribbler, the odds for a turnover increase. Here the defenders put their inside feet side by side to block the center and use their other feet to close off the baseline.

stance is the easiest thing to coach and is achieved by constant drilling and repetition. However, in the heat of play or when a player is tired, a poorly laid foundation of form is the first thing to fall apart.

The Triple-Threat Position

We've already covered the triple-threat offensive position. Well, there is also a triple-threat defensive position. (See Figure 6-6.)

In the defensive position, a player lines up one long step from the person with the ball, just far enough so the defender can reach out and touch the opponent's chest. The triple-threat posture allows the defender to move forward, sideways or vertically to stop a dribble, a pass or a shot. Triple-threat is simply the position which best allows the player to make any one of those three moves in a split second.

Setting Up the Body—The triple-threat requires the legs to be spread and the weight balanced on the front half of the feet. The body is low in a

FIGURE 6-6
TRIPLE-THREAT DEFENSE

The *triple-threat defense* provides a position from which a defender can move forward, right or left, and defend against a shot, pass or dribble.

crouch, knees bent, waist partially bent. The head is up, always. Hands are out in front of the body, spread just outside shoulder width. Palms are in or up, this is important to reduce fouls. Referees tend to call the downward hand motion a foul, but not an upward motion.

What to Watch—Many coaches teach their players to focus more on the ball handler's belly, since that's the toughest thing to fake. It's much easier to fake the eyes, head, ball and feet. I think the advice is generally good, conceptually. But a player really needs to stay in touch with the whole offensive player. The ball is what we want to get a hand on, so I say your players need to keep an eye on it. Tell them to stay low and "see" the ball, "see" the whole scene. In fact, I like to see players "track" the ball with the hand closest to it. Wherever the ball is, that hand is as close to it as possible, following it around. Then, if there is a chance for a steal or a tip, the hand will have started from the closest position. So teach your players the triple-threat, and emphasize the need to sense the

FIGURE 6-7
THE STEAL

One of the prettiest plays in basketball is a well-timed steal, although few kids try this move.

center of the ball handler's action, play the whole player and keep a hand close to the ball, moving with it.

Stealing the Ball

In youth basketball, many more passes are stolen than with experienced players. A younger player's passes are much softer and are more "tele-graphed." A youngster who is *looking to steal*, who *thinks* about getting the ball, will pick up opportunities to steal just by observing the oppo-nent's body and eye movements. However, most players don't even think about stealing the ball. They don't know how easy it is. It's a state of mind.

Sometimes the passer will let the whole world know where the ball is going; making it easy to steal. The defender wants to position himself a bit to the *ball side* of the player he is guarding, that is, the side where the ball handler is. The hand closest to the ball is extended out, ready to block a pass. Tell your players to judge how far it is from their hand to the passing lane between two offensive players. Most kids don't realize that it's just a few feet, a distance they can travel in much less time than it takes the ball to get there. The player does not have to catch the ball, it's only necessary to tip it away and then scoop it up. The body momentum will bring the player right to its bounce. (See Figure 6-7.)

The Steal Move—This move is a matter of sensing the right time. The player waits until the passer, often a point guard or off guard, begins to turn to pass. Coaches will usually advise their defense to let the player they are guarding catch a few passes, lull him into thinking there will be no steal threat. Then pick the right time and go. Obviously, if a player has exceptional quickness, if the passer is below average or if the receiver fails to move toward the pass, then steal every time. Watch out, however, because if the steal attempt fails, then the player is free and a score is more probable. Pass-stealing is like shooting: You must be able to succeed most of the time or don't try it. A coach should tell the team who the stealers are, that is, who should most actively try to steal. Others who are slower should continue to threaten passing lanes, but should focus more on defending their opponent than stealing.

Which Passes to Steal—The best passes to steal are guard to wing, or wing to corner. These passes usually occur during regular play patterns, so they can be anticipated better than others. A player can cheat a bit, getting ready for the steal when he recognizes the play.

Rebounding

Rebounding is a skill used for both offense and defense, but the fact is that most rebounds are defensive and should be if played properly. Rebounding has much more to do with position and strength than with height. Since the defender is usually inside the play between the man defended and the hoop, he is in an excellent position to box out or screen opponents from the ball.

Boxing Out—*Boxing out* is a fundamental defensive move which must be made every time the ball is shot. It involves pivoting toward the player with the back side, elbows and legs spread, keeping oneself in between the offensive player and the hoop.

It's important in boxing out to make contact with the player and move with him. The contact will rarely be called a foul unless it is flagrant. Usually, the offensive player is pushing too; so it evens out and no foul is called. Sometimes, a defender needs to hold the offensive player out away from the hoop by maintaining contact; other times it's sufficient to just momentarily bump him and move toward the hoop, particularly if more than 5 or 6 feet out. Your players should never get caught in too far under the hoop—little can be done in there. They should never let an opponent push them under the hoop, and always get a thigh or hip into the opponent to hold their ground.

Rebounding is tough business. Most players love to mix it up, bumping and leaning on opponents, underneath the hoop. Rebounders need to be hungry, and it helps to be a bit ornery. Dennis Rodman, not even 7 feet tall, is one of the greatest rebounders of all time—and wears his hair a different color each game! He is as ornery and independent a player as has ever played. *Underneath* is the world of grunts, groans, smacks and ouches. Players, especially big players, need to understand that they must be intimidating, and they need to assert themselves within the limits of the rules. I'm not suggesting foul play, and a coach never should. In the long run, it will hurt a kid's psychological development. But strong aggressive play is definitely needed underneath.

The Rebounding Jump—The rebounder jumps up, preferably straight up to avoid a foul. Don't go over another player who has better position—it's an easy foul for the referee to see.

Your players should measure their vertical jump. Have them stand near a wall and reach high, then mark the spot. Now have them leap and see how much higher the hand goes, again marking the wall. The difference between the two marks is the vertical jump. Boys in high school can vertical jump around 18 inches, girls 15 inches. Great leapers exceed 24 inches. Drills for improving vertical leap are discussed in this chapter.

Catching the Rebound—Caution players against getting into the habit of always tapping the rebound away. A well-placed tap against a bigger player may be needed, but always try to catch it. Catch it with both hands and land well, both feet spread out. Keep the ball high for an overhead outlet pass. If you must bring it down, do so with strength—elbows out, ball into the chest—and pivot quickly. A lot of hands will attack the ball, so be ready and be quick.

Nearly 75 percent of missed shots will rebound to the opposite side of the hoop, usually at an angle similar to or slightly greater than the shot angle. So if there is freedom and time to move, especially if no teammate is at the opposite side, your rebounders should head or lean that way.

Full Court Press

Very young teams do not normally press. It's often not allowed because kids have enough trouble dribbling or passing as it is. If they were allowed to press at very young ages, the ball would rarely get up court. By seventh or eighth grade, pressing is usually allowed. This applies man-to-man defense for the entire length of the court, right from the inbound pass. Usually one defender tries to pressure the inbound passer, and another stays between the other offensive guard and the ball. This forces a long, high inbound pass which is susceptible to interception. Just remember that someone has to stay back on defense and others get up court quickly in case the press fails. Figure 6-9 gives a good plan for the press.

Zone Defense

I think the rules of basketball should be changed to limit zone defenses or prohibit it, as in the pros. It's the lazy player's defense and does not involve much skill. In a zone, every defender stays in the lane area, low and high post, preventing the inside game. The offense must shoot from outside, and the kids don't really learn defense: They just clog up the lanes. It's not what the game was meant to be.

On the other hand, a zone is a much easier defense for kids to learn. Moreover, since kids don't shoot long shots very well and since the zone works best in stopping scoring in close to the basket, it works well at youth levels. Therefore, you will see coaches use it and will need to consider using it to remain competitive.

Teaching Zone Defense

Zone defenses are easy to teach, and they are effective, particularly against a good team or a team that does not have good outside shooting. Also, the vast skill differences and size differences in third through seventh graders make a zone suitable, since the zone defense does not allow one player to dominate the game. The zone defenses are usually a 1-2-2, a 2-1-2, a 1-3-1 or a 2-3. (See Figure 6-10.)

The entire zone formation should shift to the left or to the right, depending on where the ball is. Any players underneath are fronted to deny the inside pass, forcing the offense to shoot from outside.

The weakest part of the zone is the seams, the areas in between the defenders. Zone defenders are concentrating on their individual areas and not on people, so a quick pass and shot from a seam can catch a defender off guard. This is especially true in a 2-3 zone where the foul line area is usually open. The 1-3-1 stops the center jump shot and allows for good trapping, but its corners and baselines are exposed. The 1-2-2 is the favorite zone defense since it seems to minimize the weakness of other zones.

Man-to-Man Defense

A man-to-man defense, however, is a more open game, more exciting. Players are pitted against each other, one-on-one, and the skill level is more challenging. In man-to-man defense, a player guards her position's

FIGURE 6-9

FULL COURT PRESS

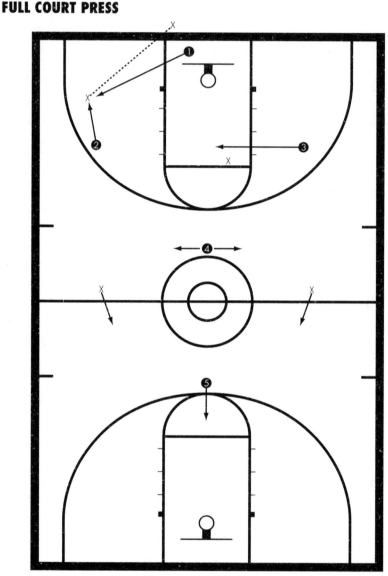

The defense lines up as shown here. #1 aggressively closes the middle, forcing the ball to be inbounded into the corner. Depending upon which side of the court the ball is inbounded from, #1 and #2 (or #3) trap the dribbler. #1 also tries to position himself to close down a passing lane. If the ball is passed back to the inbounder, trap him. The player—#2 or #3—not involved in the trap drops back into a passing lane to intercept the pass. #4 roves along the mid-court also looking to intercept a pass. #5 defends the hoop and must not let a pass get over his head.

FIGURE 6-10

ZONE DEFENSES

Zone defenses are easy to teach, and are especially effective in younger-aged teams where abilities and sizes can vary greatly. Some typical zone defenses are shown here.

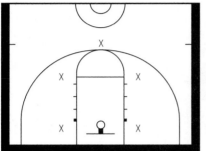

1–2–2 Zone Defense.

2–1–2 Zone Defense.

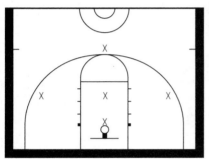

1–3–1 Zone Defense.

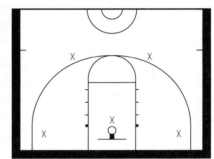

2–3 Zone Defense.

counterpart, usually matching up with a player of equal height and skill. She stays between that player and the basket at all times, whether that player has the ball or not. Kids learn more, and they know they are responsible for stopping their opponent: It's real defense. It requires better conditioning and better skills, and is a more interesting game to play and to watch. That's why the pros do it that way.

Defensive and Rebounding Drills

The Slide

Four players line up across one end of the court and slide-step sideways to the other end. The drill requires each player to take three steps toward one side and then three to the other, moving backward all the time. Coaches must ensure that players' bodies are kept low with arms out and up, that legs don't cross and that they take short quick steps.

No-Arm Shuffle

Two dribblers and two defenders start at one end of the court. Each pair should use only one-half of the court's width. The defender may not use her hands, but must endeavor to stay in front of the ball, and pressure the dribbler as they move down court. Stay low, don't cross legs, take quick short strides. The dribbler tries to lose the defender and shoot a lay-up. If the dribbler passes the defender, the defender must turn and catch up.

Rip the Screen

Four players pair up, two on offense and two on defense. The two players with the ball stand about 12 feet apart near the top of the key. They pass the ball back and forth a few times, without indicating to the defenders when or who will initiate a screen. Defenders shouldn't try to steal the passes. At some point one offensive player, after passing the ball, runs to screen his teammate's defender. The defenders must choose to switch (option A), fight through (option B), or sink back (option C). At first, practice each option, then let the players choose the right one for the play.

Rebounding

Three shooters and three rebounders stand in a semicircle 10 to 15 feet from the hoop. Use shorter distance for younger players. You, the coach, take a 15-foot shot that all players try to rebound. The defensive players must box out their man. Another good drill is for two players to practice rebounding by bouncing the ball off a wall, but make sure they don't collide with the wall.

Vertical Leap

Players should all have a spot on a wall which represents their highest leap to date, and should try to better the mark each day. Often a funny dimple in a concrete wall is enough for a marker. Players should also measure the distance between their highest reach flat-footed, and their highest point jumping. Record these statistics.

Positioning

Two players assume offensive and defensive stances out in the wing area. You stand in the key with the ball. The offensive player tries to maneuver free for a pass. The defender tries to deny him. You only pass if the offensive player gets a step on the defender.

Chapter Seven

RUNNING A PRACTICE

Perhaps the most common questions I get from coaches and parents in any sport are, "How do I start?" and "How do I run a practice?" The short answer is have players pass, defend, dribble and shoot basketballs until their arms fall off. The long answer follows.

GETTING STARTED

The job starts on day one! A month or so before the first practice, you should get the word out to your team and to their parents that things will go much better if the players show up in decent shape. Basketball doesn't require the strength of some other sports, but it does require endurance, quickness and agility. I feel it's best, particularly at grade school levels, to suggest that the players come to practice able to run a mile and to do a half-dozen 30-yard wind sprints without requiring an ambulance, and also to be able to do 25 to 50 pushups. Younger kids won't have the upper body strength, but get them started. They should do what they can, and then strive for *just one more*! This means they should work at least every other day to get up to this level.

REINFORCE THE BASICS

The other thing kids need to do early is learn the basics of the game. Kids learn to understand basketball at a pretty young age, but you shouldn't assume too much. Most importantly, tell parents about this book! Tell them to read it. It's written for parents as much as for coaches, and they can be a great help to you if they get involved early on in explaining the game and instructing their children. Finally, suggest to parents that they encourage their children to spend some time each day dribbling the ball on any hard surface. If there is a hoop around, then add in some practice with lay-ups, foul shots and jumpers. Dribbling and lay-ups are most important for beginners.

FIND EXTRA PRACTICE TIME

Unfortunately, you will probably not get as much practice time for your team as you want or need. Clinics for beginners play once or twice a week.

Club teams may practice twice and play on weekends. School teams may practice more regularly. Access to gyms is sought by all kinds of programs during winter in northern states, and so it must be shared by many. An enterprising coach can find a way to get more practice, but it's not the rule. Clearly the best practice condition is on a regulation court, but any hard surface will do for dribbling and passing as well as for conditioning. A trip to the local YMCA is an excellent alternative. Videotape scrimmages and plan an evening at someone's house to view them, maybe with some pizza. There are many ways to enrich a practice schedule, even if it's only to urge mom and dad, or big brother, to spend 30 minutes rebounding shots or mildly pressuring a player while dribbling. Advise parents as to shortcomings in their child's form so they can help make needed changes. *The more you get your players drilling their skills, the better your team will be!* That's the surest thing about any sport! A coach must find creative ways to get players more practice time. Sure, you may not be able to spend every night on it, but that's where parents, and assistant coaches, come in.

IDENTIFY YOUR GOALS

There are five key objectives you need to consider for each practice plan. Their relative importance will vary a bit as you get further into the season, and they also vary depending upon what age group you work with, but *these concepts are always important and should be part of your plan for each practice.*

Five Key Goals for Practices

1. Get the players in shape.
2. Understand each player's potential.
3. Work on individual skills and position skills.
4. Work on making them a team with sharp execution of plays and defenses.
5. Motivate, Communicate, Lead.

Basketball practices typically last for 2 to 2½ hours, depending on the day of the week and on gym availability. Grade school teams which practice daily may go for as little as an hour and a half. All five goals listed above should be considered each time you prepare a practice plan (we'll get to what a practice plan looks like a bit later). I would devote, in a 2-hour practice, 10 minutes to chatter and water breaks, 20 minutes to conditioning, 30 minutes to shooting and offensive drills, 30 minutes to defensive skills, 30 minutes to team dynamics and 30 minutes to scrimmages. Doesn't add up to 2 hours, does it? It will if you can do a few things at the same time! In fact if you have many parent-coaches helping out, you can nearly double each of these time frames.

Early in the season you should spend more time on conditioning, speed, and agility drills, and on fundamental skills such as dribbling, passing, foul shots and shooting. After a while, add in play patterns. Later in the season you need to spend more time on specialty drills and refinements.

Let's discuss each goal.

FIRST GOAL: GET THE PLAYERS IN SHAPE

Conditioning is more important in basketball than any other major sport. Frankly, it doesn't take much to get grade school or high school kids into shape; and there is just no excuse when they aren't. If you want to give your team an edge, get them in *great* shape: A lot of games are won when the other team is tired. Basketball requires endurance training, and improvement can also come from some strength training, and speed and agility drills. The worst mistake is to assume the kids will get themselves into shape. Coaches tend to underestimate the value of conditioning, but kids in shape win close games! *Even if you only get your kids to double the number of pushups they can do and run a mile regularly, they will be better players.*

There are a few do's and don'ts about getting players in shape.

Do: Warm Up

Make sure players warm up before practice. Early in the season the large muscles high on the inner thigh and groin area and the shins are vulnerable. Ankles and knees are cold if the kids just came in from outside. Most ballplayers have experienced muscular or joint strains or sprains or suffered from shin splints; these injuries can take weeks to heal. Tell your players that muscles are like bubble-gum. Unless they stretch slowly, they will tear. A half dozen laps around the gym at a slow pace should break a sweat and warm up major leg muscles. Tell them to run backward and shuffle-step part of the time. Lay-up lines do the same.

Warm-ups should occur before your practice starting time, so tell players to arrive a few minutes early. Don't expect players to warm up sufficiently on their own. They should be told to stretch out on their own before practice, but you should warm up the team together. Players who aren't warmed-up get hurt too easily.

Quick Cali Set

Start the team off with what I call the *Quick Cali Set*: 25 jumping jacks, 25 pushups, 15 half sit-ups, a dozen toe touches with legs crossed and 20 trunk turns.

Stretches

Then do the *Leg Stretch Set*. Leg stretches should be done smoothly without jerking or straining. A few good ones are:

1. *Toe-hand:* Lie on the back with arms stretched outward, on the floor. Alternately bring each foot up and over to the opposite hand.
2. *Hurdler:* Sit on the ground with one leg forward and one bent backward. Touch the forward toe, then slowly lean back to stretch the back leg. Reverse legs and repeat.
3. *Standing Quadriceps:* Standing on one leg, lift the other foot from behind to touch the buttocks. Do a half dozen for each leg.
4. *Supine Hamstring:* Lying on the back with hands behind one knee, pull that leg, as straight legged as possible, to the chest. Repeat with the other one. No jerking movements, no bobbing up and down!
5. *Thigh Stretch:* Standing with legs outstretched sideways, lean to one side, bending that knee, to stretch the opposite thigh muscle.
6. *Achilles and Calf Stretch:* Place one foot a step in front of the other. Lean forward and bend the front leg, stretching the lower part of the back leg. Switch legs.

Jumping

Players should also do some jumping warm-ups. A good one is to hop a few times on one foot, squat on both feet and touch the floor; hop a few times on the other foot, squat again, then burst up in a two-legged full high jump. Jumping rope is also an excellent warm-up, and improves jumping ability and agility. After this, they should pair up and shoot fouls or work on an individual skill you have advised them to improve upon until you are ready to start practice.

Do: Start on Time!

Late-comers catch up and do an additional 20 pushups. The team captain can lead the warm-up exercises while you get organized, check to see who is there, and talk to coaches or parents. (See Figure 7-1.)

Do: Monitor Your Players

Don't overwork players! Some coaches have their kids running all the time all season long. The players are young, but there are limits even for the

FIGURE 7-1

WARM UPS

The hurdler is a good method for stretching the legs. A player sits on the ground with one left forward and the other bent back. He touches the big toe of the extended foot, then slowly leans back to stretch the bent leg.

A good thigh stretch technique is to stand with the legs spread sideways, then lean to one side, bending the knee. This stretches the opposite thigh muscle.

To stretch the quadricep while standing, stand on one leg while pulling the other leg up behind the buttocks.

To stretch the Achilles, hamstring and calf muscles, cross one foot with the other and lean forward to stretch the upper and lower rear muscles in the back leg.

young. By the same token, there might be periods when players are just standing around. Here are some exercises players can do when they have free time during a practice.

Strength Enhancers

I believe that pushups are the best single exercise for building upper body strength in kids (along with the hated situps). Hand out sets of 20 pushups or sit-ups freely. Another great strength enhancer is the *wrist machine*, as I call it. It's simply a two-foot section of broom handle or thick pipe with four feet of clothesline attached to the center and a 5 to 10 pound weight attached to the other end of the line. Hold the bar with arms outstretched, and coil or roll the bar and the line around it until the weight rises to reach the bar. Then lower it and do it twice more. It's great for wrists and forearms, and leads to the ability to pass crisply. I had kids work on it when not engaged in a scrimmage. Stress to your players that these exercises will give them an edge they will need when they come up against their opponents. If a kid does a hundred pushups a day, he will become very strong! Judge what a player can do, and slightly push his limit. Don't ask him to do something that will embarrass him, however.

Don't: Encourage Formal Weight Training

I generally recommend avoiding formal weight training for grade school kids since they are still growing at a rapid pace. However, there is a different view, and I'll present it in chapter nine, on formal conditioning.

Don't: Do Wind Sprints, Until the *End* of Practice

Wind sprints require the loosest muscles, so they should normally be done at the end of practice. Even then keep them short: 10 to 20 yards at first, working up to 30.

The *suicide drill* is a great sprint drill for ending practice. The kids start at an end line, sprint to the top of the key, touch the floor, and sprint back and touch the floor. Then they sprint to half-court in the same manner. They finish up with the downcourt key and finally a full court sprint. The whole exercise involves eight sprints. Time them! Tell the players to reach out in a long stride. Do some backward and some sideways.

Finish practice with a few half-court races. Wind sprints are essential for endurance and leg strength. If they are waiting for their parents, remind them that foul shots are hardest to shoot when very tired, and the best time to get a few in is after sprints.

Speed and Leaping Improvement Drills

You can't do much to make a slow kid a lot faster; but you can improve speed somewhat, and you can improve running *strength*, agility and balance by a good deal.

Some good drills to improve running speed and form are:

The Robot

Line up the players and have them run full-court at half speed, alternatively driving their fists downward from neck-height to just behind the buttocks. The idea is to bang or drive the fists downward in a robotic cadence in rhythm with their stride. The arms are bent to start but can be straightened into whatever position is comfortable. Look at track stars in the 100-yard dash, and observe how they pump the arms. Have players run it three times, increasing speed each time.

The Bounce

This is similar to the robot, except players concentrate on lifting their knees high as possible toward the chest, bouncing off the ground with each step. This drill, routinely done by track stars and high jumpers, develops the power thrust needed to sprint. Try to incorporate the robot drill with this one after a while.

The Buttkick

Again run 40 yards and return, this time kicking the heels into the buttocks. This helps the follow-through needed for a complete stride. Players need every bit of thrust to sprint.

The Goose Step

Finally, run 40 yards in a *goose step*, kicking the legs straight out and lifting them vertically and high. This drill develops a greater stride.

Agility Drills

Simon Says

Line up players in five lines. The first row of five start running in place, body low, short, quick, choppy steps. Using your hand, signal the players to shuffle laterally (without crossing the feet), forward, backward and downward to the ground. Players must square the shoulders, stay low and react quickly. Slow reacting players who don't appear to be trying hard enough may be rewarded with a dozen pushups. Go for twenty seconds and then repeat the drill a new row of players.

Carioca

Lined up as for the Simon Says drill, players carioca, that is, run sideways, left foot *over* right, then left foot *behind* right, for 40 yards. Repeat four times.

Putting Drills Into Practice

I usually divide the team into two groups for drills, guards in one and forwards and centers in another. I start with defensive drills, and then do offensive drills. Then we just shoot for a while. Kids love this part of practice. It's better to have them shooting when they are a bit tired already.

Let the kids know that drills are done so that skills become automatic and will be there for them under pressure. Let them know the objective of each drill, what skill you are looking to improve. I believe it's better to keep drills short and fast-paced. Several repetitions for each player are enough. Better to use multiple drills than wear one out. By mid-season you want conditioning and skills drills compacted so they take less time. Later in this chapter I'll provide a plan for what I call "stations" to help with this.

SECOND GOAL: UNDERSTAND EACH PLAYER'S POTENTIAL

You need to figure out what each player can do, so he can concentrate on developing the specific skills needed in his position.

Generally bigger kids play underneath, and smaller kids are guards, but not necessarily. Some big kids have remarkable ball handling and passing skills, and these should be developed. Some average-sized kids have great leaping ability and have a knack at getting into position for rebounds. So, keep an open mind, and figure out what players you need to move around a bit. I've seen many coaches decide too quickly who plays where and then never change it. I have also seen a coach stick someone in an odd position, late in a meaningless game, and suddenly find that the kid was a natural there. While it's important to get things set early in order to concentrate on the special skills required by each position, you should always be looking to see if a player could help the team somewhere else. Assistant coaches can help you a lot here. Some kids are lousy at practice and come alive in a game; some are opposite and can't do it under pressure.

Keep Track of Players' Strengths

A good way to do this is to start making lists. Run sprints to see who your fastest players are. Who can accelerate the best, that is, has the best short-distance time? Who are the most agile? Who are the risk-takers, the fiercest defenders, the strongest players? Who has the best hands? Who wants the ball the most? Who are the natural leaders? Who has a three-point shot, a jumper, a great foul shot percentage? Who can dribble, pass, follow play patterns to the letter?

118

Once you create these lists, don't throw them away. Check them every couple of weeks, and see if someone has earned another look. The lists are helpful since they force you to evaluate your players according to different aspects of athletic ability. Sometimes you will be surprised to see a name pop up whom you hadn't been looking at very closely.

Constantly evaluate and reevaluate your players. It's incredible to me how rarely some coaches will discuss each player. It is simply far too easy to oversee a quiet kid who may have good ability. Perhaps an assistant coach usually has seen something that can surface in a full review. Don't just label someone for the season. Reconsider constantly. Give a kid a shot at something else if he is not working out where you first placed him.

Talk With Your Players

You will find many brief opportunities on the gym floor to talk to your players. How is school? Does she seem troubled or angry? How are things at home? What are your interests? You can find out a lot about a kid in just a few minutes to help you understand the player, and you will also begin to earn her respect. Kids who like and respect you are more coachable.

THIRD GOAL: WORK ON INDIVIDUAL SKILLS

After 25 minutes (less in mid-season) of conditioning, stretching and speed and agility drills, I like to call the players together and give them an overview of what they will be doing in practice and what we expect of them. You might post the practice plan, so they know what's coming. Details can be supplied later.

The drills for individual development are generally found in chapters two, three and four. I won't repeat them here, but will list them in the sample practice plan near the end of this chapter.

Videotape Practices

Focus practice at first on individual form, skills and fundamentals. I think it's a great idea to film kids at practice. Try to get a parent to volunteer to take some shots of players working on form and shooting, as well as running drills. Circulate the tapes to kids who need to see what they are doing wrong. You can all meet at someone's house to view the films and talk about form. In coaching as in art, a picture is truly worth a thousand words.

Working on form and fundamentals early in the season on a regular basis is *essential*, and videotapes will help you here. Good form will go a long way, rely upon it! If a shooter leans back too far or has poor wrist and hand form, if a guard is not passing to open space, if a low triple-threat posture is not being used or if forwards don't box out, let them know. *There is no excuse for poor form!* A player may not be able to hit every shot, or execute every play pattern well, but he can *always employ proper form*, and form alone will help! Have the checklist at the end of the book handy to check a player's form.

FOURTH GOAL: TEAMWORK PRACTICE

The last half hour or so of practice is a good time to get the whole team together for drills which require two full teams on the floor. For teamwork drills, players should generally be assigned to their regular positions, once those positions have been established. The drills covering team play and play patterns, listed in the Practice Plan later in this chapter, are generally found in chapters five and six.

Early in the preseason this part of practice can be skipped since you need to focus on fundamentals and conditioning above all: Gradually you will work up to about an hour during mid-season for teamwork, including a scrimmage.

Scrimmages are fun for the kids, and even 15 minutes at the end of practice is a good idea. However, in the first weeks of preseason they have much to learn, and there will be little time for anything extended.

FIFTH GOAL: MOTIVATE, COMMUNICATE, LEAD

I devote much of chapter eight to this topic, but I'll preview the concept here. Many coaches seem to spend a lot of time hollering, trying to motivate players, and to get them to increase their concentration.

Frankly, whereas energy is sometimes great and you have to yell to be heard, the screamer routine is often quite overdone. Furthermore, there is a line that shouldn't be crossed, and that is humiliating a player. The idea is to be firm, to let players know that they can do better if they focus a bit more.

Ask yourself what your ultimate goal is. To win? To help a young boy or girl learn how to face challenges? If the latter is at least a significant part of your reason for coaching, then try the positive reinforcement methods described in chapter eight. Stress that he needs to be more productive to get more playing time. Coach a kid according to *his* needs—some need caring, some need a gentle boot in the can, some need patience.

Most importantly, reward good effort. Praise good hustle. Yell out, "That's basketball!" It can get infectious. You are the leader of the team, the most significant person out there. What do you want their memory of you to be?

THE PRACTICE PLAN

Each practice should follow a written practice plan. It just takes a few minutes to think through what you want to accomplish, and it does wonders for efficient use of time. A practice plan follows a general routine. It varies somewhat in the proportion of time spent on areas as the season moves along, and the actual drills used (mix them up for variety).

During the first weeks in the season your plan should focus on (1) conditioning, (2) individual skills development, (3) evaluating your players and (4) "homework" time spent looking at play patterns. Then the plan's focus shifts to team dynamics, and specialty plays. Note that I said *focus—all of these concepts are involved in every practice all year.*

The following are typical sample practice plans for different weeks during a season. The major segments of each plan are usually the same. First you do conditioning, then defensive skills practice, offensive skills practice, shooting practice and team dynamics. Finish with sprints and closing comments. Most non-school teams start at 6:00 P.M. during the weekdays, since coaches at grade school levels have day jobs. Some of you will be able to start right after school. This practice plan is for two hours. If you have two and a half hours then expand sessions according to what's needed at a given point in the season. The following plan is a tight one. Players need to hustle from drill to drill. Coaching should be crisp. Nearly everything is done at top speed. Monitor the pace, and give a breather here or there as needed.

On the last page of this chapter is a blank practice plan which you can copy. You can waste a lot of time if you are not organized, and can triple the value of the practice if you are.

First Weeks of Preseason: Practice Plan

TIME	ACTIVITY
Early birds	Run laps: forward, backward, shuffle. Jumping and vertical leap drills. Foul shots, individual moves work. Vision therapy drills.
6:00 P.M.	**CONDITIONING:** Quick cali set, leg stretch set.
	SPEED DRILLS: Robot, bounce, buttkick, goosestep.
	AGILITY DRILLS: Simon says, carioca.
	JUMPING DRILLS.
6:25 P.M.	Call team together. Brief comments.
6:30 P.M.	**DEFENSIVE SKILLS PRACTICE:** Coach demonstrates triple-threat form, deny-pass form (low post and high post) and rebound form. Then split into two groups at either end. Do *No Arm Shuffle* and *Three-*

Man Rebound. At another practice introduce the *Rip the Screen.* After a week or two introduce the *Three-on-Two-on-One.*

6:50 P.M.   **WATER BREAK.**

7:00 P.M.   **OFFENSIVE SKILLS PRACTICE:** Each day coaches demonstrate one or two areas of form: triple-threat offensive form; jump shot form (particularly jump straight and high, cradle high, wrist form); dribbling form; passing form (chest, bounce, overhead, etc.); boxing out; lay-up. Then break into two groups and do a drill dedicated to that subject.

7:30 P.M.   **SHOOTING PRACTICE:** Drills such as *21 Jumper, 21 Lay-up* and *50 Freebies.* After a few days let players shoot from their optimum location. Each player needs to find and know their range.

7:50 P.M.   **SPRINTS, RACES, "SUICIDES."**

8:00 P.M.   **CLOSING COMMENTS,** practice over.

           POST-PRACTICE: Foul shots till parent comes.

Midway Between First Practice and First Game: Saturday Practice Plan

TIME   ACTIVITY

Early birds   Run laps: forward, backward, shuffle. Jumping and vertical leap drills. Foul shots, individual moves work. Vision therapy drills.

11:00 A.M.   **CONDITIONING:** Quick cali set, leg stretch set.

           SPEED DRILLS: Robot, bounce, buttkick, goosestep.

           JUMPING DRILLS.

11:15 A.M.   Call team together. Brief comments.

11:20 A.M.   **DEFENSIVE SKILLS PRACTICE:** Split into two groups at either end. Do one drill, *No Arm Shuffle, Three-Man Rebound* or *Rip the Screen,* for ten minutes. Do *Three-on-Two-on-One* for ten minutes. Observe form fundamentals, use checklist.

11:40 A.M.   **WATER BREAK.**

11:45 A.M.   **OFFENSIVE SKILLS PRACTICE:** Split into two groups. Do one dribbling, one shooting, then one passing drill for seven minutes each.

12:05 P.M.   **SHOOTING PRACTICE:** Drills such as *21 Jumper, 21 Lay-up* or *50 Freebies.* Let players focus on their best shot, and take a step beyond their range to see how it's improving.

12:20 P.M.   **TEAM PRACTICE:** Break squad up into two even teams. Walk through key play patterns, e.g., *Shuffle, Wheel, Pick and Roll.* Slowly apply light defense in a day or so, increasing gradually to full defense.

12:45 P.M. **SPECIALTY PRACTICE:** Each day introduce one specialty drill such as: *Inbounding* (*under yours, sideline, under theirs*), *Center Tap, Fast Break, Breaking the Press.*

12:55 P.M. **SCRIMMAGE:** Be sure players not involved are working on something useful.

1:20 P.M. **SPRINTS, RACES, "SUICIDES."**

1:30 P.M. **CLOSING COMMENTS,** practice over.

POST-PRACTICE: Foul shots till parent comes.

Mid-Season: Evening Practice Plan

TIME   ACTIVITY

Early birds Run laps: forward, backward, shuffle. Jumping and vertical leap drills. Foul shots, individual moves work.

6:00 P.M. **CONDITIONING:** Quick cali set, leg stretch set.

JUMPING DRILLS.

6:10 P.M. Call team together. Brief comments.

6:15 P.M. **DEFENSIVE SKILLS PRACTICE:** Do *Three-on-Two-on-One.*

6:30 P.M. **OFFENSIVE SKILLS PRACTICE:** *Crisscross; Stop, Pivot, Go;* and *Cuts.*

6:50 P.M. **SHOOTING PRACTICE:** Drills such as *21 Jumper, 21 Lay-up,* and *50 Freebies.* Let players focus on their best shot, and take a step beyond their range to see how it's improving.

7:05 P.M. **WATER BREAK.**

7:10 P.M. **SCRIMMAGE:** First team against subs. Practice. Run the offense.

7:50 P.M. **SPRINTS, RACES, "SUICIDES."**

8:00 P.M. **CLOSING COMMENTS,** practice over.

POST-PRACTICE: Foul shots till parent comes.

ADJUSTING THE PLAN FOR BEGINNERS

These plans work well for most age groups. At younger ages, you can shorten the conditioning a bit, and spend some time talking basketball. Get them in a circle and ask them questions: "What's a foul?" "What's a walk or a double dribble?" "Who can name the floor positions?" "What's a lay-up?" "A jump shot?" "A hook or a three-pointer?" "What is meant by 'three seconds'?" "What are the various names for things around the court?"

Gather them all around the key and demonstrate proper stance and shooting form. Tell them about bad form. Demonstrate defensive form. When coaching beginners, it's important to spend a fair amount of time on this each practice until they start to get a feel for the jargon and the rules of basketball. Use the glossary in the back of this book. After a while, you'll know when they get it.

At young ages it will take longer to teach drills, but make sure you acquaint the players with every concept, and walk through drills.

SETTING UP STATIONS

One final word about specialty drills and parents. I once had seven parents, men and women, on the court helping out. I had fourteen kids on the team. I set up what we called *stations*, a group of simultaneous drills on separate areas of the court. It's a technique I used often while coaching soccer. The drills are competitive, so keep scores to see who does the best. Each drill lasts for five minutes, then the kids rotate to the next station until they have each performed all seven stations. Here are the individual stations:

Cone Dribbling

One parent sets up a half dozen cones along a sideline, 4 to 5 feet apart. Players take turns dribbling between and around each cone. Time the dribbling for a round trip. See who has the fastest time.

One-on-One

Another parent supervises a one-on-one match at a basket. Keep score.

Three-Point Shots

One parent supervises two players shooting three-pointers and getting their own rebounds.

12-Foot Jump Shots

One parent supervises two shooting jumpers. Again, count the total shots made. Players get their own rebounds.

Two Ball Pass Drill

A parent supervises two players in the two ball pass drill.

Hit the Spot

A parent takes two players to a wall area where they try to hit a spot on the wall from 12 feet out. Each player gets her own spot! Mix up chest passes, bounce passes and two-hand overhead passes equally. Count the number of direct hits on the spot.

Two Tap

A parent supervises two players 4 to 5 feet apart who tap the ball to each other, trying to keep it in the air. Count the number of successive taps.

That's it. I rotated them from station to station, 35 minutes for the whole deal. The kids got the equivalent experience of seven single-coach practices! You can make the exercise longer and design your own stations. If I had two more kids and a parent, I would have done some vision therapy drills also (see chapter nine).

DAILY PRACTICE SCHEDULE

DAY_____

TIME   ACTIVITY

_____   _____

_____   _____

_____   _____

_____   _____

_____   _____

_____   _____

_____   _____

_____   _____

_____   _____

_____   _____

NOTES _____

_____

_____

_____

_____

Chapter Eight

THE PSYCHOLOGY OF COACHING

Aren't they too young to learn all this? Will the competition, the emphasis on winning, be too much at certain ages or for certain types of kids? How do you motivate a rambunctious 10-year-old? How do you get kids to play with consistency? What is a good age to start?

DON'T UNDERESTIMATE YOUR PLAYERS

If your players—or your son or daughter—are very young (less than nine), then it will be a few years before the more technical parts of the game will be understood well enough to routinely occur on the court. But all of it, including the more complicated concepts such as continuous patterns, pick and roll, fast break—all of it, should be taught, or at least covered, at all ages. Don't underestimate your players. Some of them will grasp these concepts. The basics, especially dribbling, passing and shooting, should be emphasized right away before bad habits form. However, a lot of the refinements such as the *defending the screen, multiple fakes* and *switching* take time and maturity.

It's your job to get them started. Someone has to start so the next year's coach can build on it. Maybe if parents and coaches set the stage in the very early years, refinements could happen in grade school. But if your players are green, don't worry about it, concentrate on the basics, cover the advanced stuff, but don't expect too much too soon.

IT TAKES TIME AND PATIENCE

Believe me when I say there is no magic age. Look at kids mastering moves in gymnastics, soccer and other sports at seven and eight years old. It's not that younger kids can't learn. They just need someone who understands refined concepts and has the time and ability to teach them.

It largely depends on how much time you have to practice, and unfortunately that's the biggest problem. We all have many obligations, and youth sports usually can't be practiced every day. Do what you can! There isn't anything in this book that's over their heads. Just start somewhere, and the kids will absorb as much as you have the time and patience to teach them.

Some skills will take a few sessions, some require much more, some will take years, but it will happen. Like learning how to whistle, suddenly one day it's there, and you sense it was always really simple to do.

THE COACH-PLAYER RELATIONSHIP

The relationship between a coach and a player is a powerful one. You are not only a father (or mother!) figure, but you are the final authority in what is, in his or her mind, the most important thing in life.

Through his athletic experiences, a kid finds out things about himself— good or bad—and he will always associate those things with you. Coaching is as an awesome responsibility. You may want to ignore this larger picture, but sticking your head in the sand does not change what's really going on. This book provides many tools you can use to help you make the experience a good one, whether you win or lose as a team, but in the final analysis it comes down to whether you really give a darn enough to accept the larger role of being both a coach and a friend.

Most of your players will never make cuts at the high school level, a few may play in college, but you will probably never coach a future pro basketball player. However, every one of your players will become an adult someday, with the responsibility of a job and probably a family as well. The whole idea of youth sports is to provide valuable life lessons. It is doubtful that they will remember much about this season twenty years from now, certainly not the scores of various games. But I guarantee you one thing. They will remember you for the rest of their lives. The memory of my coaches is etched clearly in my mind. I remember them vividly, for good or for bad. You may not remember all of the kids you coached, particularly if you do it for a number of years, but every one of them will remember you. How do you want to be remembered?

ON WINNING

Our society is ferociously competitive in spirit. Pressuring children too hard may turn them into adults so obsessed with being first that they get no joy out of life except in the narrow field of competition. They neither give nor get pleasure in their relationships with spouses, children, friends, and fellow workers.

Dr. Benjamin Spock

128

Basketball is like a war! . . . Winning comes first!

Red Auerbach, Coach, General Manager, President, Boston Celtics

Feelings on the importance of winning run strong. As with religion and politics, everyone thinks they are right. Vince Lombardi, the legendary coach of the Packers football team, once said, "Winning isn't everything . . . it's the only thing." There are still coaches who will tell you that, if you are going to keep score, you should try to win.

Let's face it, if you tell kids winning is no big deal, they may blankly nod, but they won't buy it. They *know* about winning. They know the guys on the other team will gloat and taunt them back at school. They know about trophies and news articles. They hear the empty silence after a loss, the lectures from the coach: They feel the pressure.

Well, the truth of it is somewhere in between. Kids talk about winning, but I believe that, down deep, they care as much or even more about how well they are doing personally. Many of you will remember in your playing days, a game where the team won but you didn't contribute. Was that satisfactory? Or how about a game where the team lost, but you had a super day? How did you feel? Sure you wanted to win. Sure it's a team sport. But the personal satisfaction went a long way toward easing the pain.

All right, winning is important in the pro's. Maybe it becomes important even for some kids in high school, since scholarship money rarely looks at anybody on a team with a 3 to 26 record. But in youth basketball, it's just not as important. Parents and coaches may think it is, but the kids often forget the game and certainly the score as soon as they get home.

What they *will* remember however is how they feel about themselves, and how you reacted. Practical advice? I tell my kids something they can believe, that winning is never important in youth basketball, but that it is always fun to win. That's the truth. They can relate to it. I tell them what's important is how they handle victory or defeat; that it's important to try to be as good as they can be, to help each other and to try to do their best. We try to win, but all we can really control is how hard we try.

BALANCE YOUR NEEDS

At the heart of how good a coach you will be is how well you balance your need to win with the need to develop healthy young people. This balance will affect your every action, your relationship with each player and the atmosphere on the court. It will characterize the memory of your coaching experience for many years to come. Striking that balance involves a continuing struggle between the passions fired up by competition, and the caring you feel for your players as a responsible adult. A basketball game will stir up some powerful emotions. It's said that winning builds character, while losing reveals it. Competitive fire can quickly melt an otherwise cool, calm, collected attitude.

HOW TO FIND YOUR BALANCE

I often found my own balance in light of how much talent we had on the team. When I saw we had little chance of winning it all, I chose to emphasize individual goals. Let's face it, if you can't get there, there is absolutely no sense in getting everyone crazy. But when you have a potential championship team . . . that's the real test!

The point is *it is a balance*. Winning and development are both part of the game. For instance, we may worry about the total dedication required of young Olympic athletes, having sacrificed much of their youth for their quest. Yet, we know they have enjoyed moments of glory which seem to transcend life itself, achieving heights most of us only dream about.

SO MUCH FOR EXPERTS

It's just not realistic and certainly not helpful to have "experts" like Alfie Kohn tell us in his book *No Contest: The Case Against Competition* (Houghton Mifflin) that years of psychological research prove that "competition is poison." That is like telling us not to breathe because the air is polluted! Competition is a part of life, period!

I don't think the proper balance was found by Eric Margenau, a renowned sports psychologist who, in *Sports Without Pressure* (Gardner Press, 1990), suggested that "Competition is fine, but should be kept friendly. . . . Parents should not pressure a child to excel *regardless of that child's abilities.*" I disagree. Lets face it. We all know kids who could excel but don't, kids who just need a good boot in the backside to get going.

COMPETITION BRINGS OUT THE WORST IN SOME

By the same token, many of us will remember the ugly scene on national TV when irresistible competitive fires drove Ohio State coaching legend Woody Hayes to assault an opposing Clemson player on the field. And we cringed when young tennis star Mary Pierce, symbolic of many troubled young athletes, had to obtain a restraining order against her father, who had been pressuring her. The frenzy to win, riding upon the dark horse of fear of failure, can and does get both crazy and destructive!

COMPETITION IS PART OF LIFE

The issue of competition goes to the essence of the human condition: It is part of our evolution. Its answers are complex and most elusive. After many years of coaching and playing sports, to me the clearest answer is to not give up. I recently read in the *New York Times* that some schools are abandoning competitive interaction in their phys ed programs to avoid damaging feelings of kids who are not outstanding. Isn't it better that kids learn about and prepare for success and failure in a controlled setting, inside the relatively harmless gymnasium, than in the crucible of adult life?

Should we abandon competition, and with it the struggle to succeed, just because we, as a society, haven't always done it right? We couldn't quit if we wanted to. It's part of life and we must continue to work to find the best balance.

WINNING AND GROWTH

Winning and growth do share a common ground. Coaches who win consistently are often remembered by their former players more for the great lessons of life than for the gold cup on the mantle.

These coaches know that the key to success is in motivating athletes to win the personal struggles to do their best and to improve beyond apparent limitations, spurred on by their team's goals. These coaches know that the *spirit,* the *will to win,* the *will to excel* are the important things that transcend the game itself.

How you resolve the balance between winning and individual development is up to you. If you recognize the need to strike a balance you are off to a good start. My own approach in coaching is probably best characterized as a back-and-forth struggle to maintain that balance. When I find myself too focused on the win, I step back a bit. I remind myself that while we're going for it, we need to stay on the high road.

Every coach has felt the gut-wrenching that stays with you for hours after a game. I think it's enough to be honest about the reality of competitive passion, and then commit yourself to doing what you expect of your players—doing your best with it!

I believe most coaches want to try to build character and create a positive experience for each player, *and* win the game. There are some who never really challenge their teams for fear of upsetting the kids, and these "nice guys" don't do much damage. Of course their players may never make it to the next level of play. Other coaches feel compelled to win at any cost, and the cost can be tragic for the fragile psyche of a young boy or girl.

Find the middle ground. If you can't deal with the pressure, then consider whether coaching is right for you (and for the kids).

Use Reality Checks

Parents talk to each other about how they feel and how their kids are feeling. One practical way to get a "reality check" is to pick out a parent who seems to know the other parents well and ask her how the parents think things are going. She may offer insight into general problems or even problems related to a specific child that no parent would ever tell you directly.

Of course, the balance between winning and building character seem to vary with the age of your team. At preteen levels, the most emphasis is usually placed on developing the individual. This doesn't mean that winning is not an issue: It's just not at all important. The focus is on development. This is why most programs require that all kids play a minimal amount of time. By high school varsity play, the balance between winning and growth becomes more even. It should never get further than that, but the reality of major collegiate play is that losing coaches don't last.

ON MOTIVATION

Rock, I know I'm going to die. I'm not afraid. But someday, Rock, when things on the field are going against us, tell the boys, Rock, to go out there and win just one for the Gipper. Now, I know where I'll be then, coach. But I'll know about it, and I'll be happy.

George Gipp

OK, it's a football story, but it's the best motivation story there is. Legendary Notre Dame coach Knute Rockne waited eight years until, during halftime in a big game against Army, he repeated these last words of his dying quarterback in what was to become the epitome of halftime motivation.

It's a beautiful story, but coaches need to rely upon a lot more than speeches to motivate their team. Sure, some coaches have that charismatic quality and can motivate a team just by the sheer strength of their personality. Indiana coach Bobby Knight is perhaps the best example.

However, the rest of us "mere mortal" guys need to consider motivational techniques that can help us get the job done. The "secrets" of good motivation are easily found in the growing science of *sports psychology*. Once considered mere gobbledygook, the mental aspect of competition is now a cornerstone of athletic development at the highest levels of amateur and professional sports. Many teams, including the U.S. Olympic program, have employed full-time sports psychologists.

It is not the purpose of this book to go into the psychology of sports in great depth. You will find aspects of psychology spread throughout this book as well as my books on coaching other youth sports. I have used psychological insight throughout my 20 years of coaching, and you will probably agree that much of this is common sense, obvious to any caring adult. My *checklist* approach to teaching correct form is consistent with the mental checklist sports psychologists urge athletes to use. If you want to focus more deeply on this area, one of the best books I've read on this subject was *The Athlete's Guide to Sports Psychology: Mental Skills for Physical People* by Dorothy V. Harris, Ph.D. and Bette L. Harris, Ed.D. (Leisure Press, 1984). I will, however, discuss some emerging motivational techniques that seem to work best.

Attaboy!

There never will be a better tool than frequent positive reinforcement for young athletes. It is essential to liberally give out some *attaboys* (or *attagirls*) for good effort.

In *Kidsports: A Survival Guide for Parents* (Addison-Wesley, 1983), Dr. Nathan J. Smith, a consultant for the American Board of Pediatrics, studied two groups of coaches. He found that "the single most important difference in our research between coaches to whom young athletes respond most favorably and those to whom they respond least favorably was the frequency with which coaches reinforce and reward desirable behavior."

A pat on the back, a smile, clapping, praise, a wink and a nod, as well as tangible rewards such as mention in the newspaper article, more playing time—all go a very long way toward motivating high performance. I would add to this concept that the rewards are even more effective when they emphasize outstanding effort as opposed to a great result. An athlete has complete control over the amount of effort he puts into his game. The result however is dependent on many things, many of which are beyond the individual's control. Even corrective action, pointing out mistakes, should be sandwiched somehow within some positive comments; e.g., "Good try, Jack. Next time get a better shot—you can do it!"

Don't Be a Coach Who Loses It

Coaches spend a lot of time hollering, trying to motivate players, trying to get them to increase their energy level and to develop that all-important *desire to perform.* However, we often see coaches lose it, and cross the line of tolerable motivation. The idea is to be firm, to let players know that they can do better if they reach deeper into their gut. I like to ask players if they gave it their best. *"Was that your best effort?" "Is that all you have to give?"*

Focus on the Effort

Let a player know what you think about his *effort*, not *himself.* Don't personalize it—the kid is a decent person. Focus on the effort during practice. A kid can relate to trying harder, but he can't relate positively to your telling him he stinks.

Explain the problem with fundamentals or form so he *understands the concept.* Take the time he needs to get the idea.

Most importantly, reward good effort openly and liberally. Praise a good steal. Recognize hustle. Yell out, "That's basketball!" It can get infectious.

Having one set of standards for everyone doesn't mean you shouldn't handle players differently. Some kids respond well when you correct them in front of their peers. Others are devastated when you get on them. Take these kids aside, sit down with them, and find out what's going on in their lives; see if you can learn what the problem is.

We Are Family!

I've read the autobiographies of many great coaches. One constant in all of their stories is their ability to relate to the different individuals on their team, to create a family-type environment. Each kid is different, and each one needs a personal approach. Most importantly, even the lowest substitute should be treated with equal respect to the best players.

I used to start each season with a team discussion on what it means to be on a team. One thing I would tell the players is that for the rest of the season they are all friends. They are all in a special relationship with each other. I tell them they should say hello in the school hallways, and help each other off the court, if needed. I never tolerated criticism of a teammate on the court, and would quickly bench any offender. Kids were expected to urge each other on, to quickly tell a teammate to put a mistake behind him. I promoted team dinners and outings, and moved to break up cliques.

Team building is a proven ticket to success. The concept is widely used in all walks of life, and is a staple of Japanese and American business organization. *It doesn't just happen because a bunch of kids are on a team.* It happens when coaches work at it. Team building is actually quite easy to get done; just put it in the practice plan, talk to your assistant coaches about it, and opportunities to promote *teamness* will present themselves in abundance.

Set Realistic Goals

It may seem trite to say, but setting realistic goals is essential to proper motivation, for the team and for each individual. With specific goals, a kid has something clear and achievable to work on, something she can set her sights on. She is not responsible for the whole team, nor for winning or losing. She is not overwhelmed and defeated by unrealistic expectations.

Goals Provide Stimulation

I think it's a good idea to have each player set his own goals under your guidance. I usually offer the players a number of categories in which a few goals should be set.

One category is conditioning, and the goals may be to double the number of pushups he can do, knock a number of seconds off a mile or a 100-yard sprint, or increase his pull-ups.

A second goal category relates to specific skills for his position. It may be to improve the form of his shot or his defensive stance.

A third goal category relates to game performance, for example, the number of rebounds. I might also suggest to a player that he work on his self-confidence, his self-control, his relationship with certain teammates or his effort at practice. I'll have this written down by the player, and we'll occasionally review progress. Don't set too many, just focus on key areas.

ON PEAK PERFORMANCE

The bane of coaches is whatever it is that makes a kid play great one day and completely fall apart the next. A kid misses his first five shots, and he winds up walking around in a daze all day. Another kid makes a good steal, and suddenly starts to terrorize the court. One day the guard can't pass to save his life. Other days his play seems transcendent.

The Fight or Flight Instinct

Modern science tells us that how we cope with the stress of the challenge is all "upstairs," at least much of it. Mental control, or its lack, begins with the commonly known "fight or flight" instinct, that is, the natural impulse that arises in cornered animals to respond to a threat by fighting it or fleeing from it. It is a genetic reaction, which as humans we inherited from our earliest ancient ancestors.

There's not a kid alive who hasn't felt those butterflies in the stomach. This reaction under game conditions can create a panic that distracts concentration and may even cause muscle spasms. However, when controlled properly, it can lead the athlete to a "zone" of peak performance.

Studies Explain What Happens

In the February 14, 1994, issue of *U.S. News and World Report*, an article entitled "The Inner Game of Winning" reported on the research of Stanford University neurobiologist Robert Sapolsky. He found that the properly controlled response to challenge causes a desirable increase in adrenaline and sugar, producing the sense of "heightened awareness and flow" associated with being in a peak "zone." The negative counterpart, which he calls the "fearful" response, produces a bodily cocktail laced with a substance called *cortisol*, which can "not only impair performance, but can also lead over the long run to damage the arteries and liver and lead to depression."

Another interesting study, "The Mental Edge: The Brain Is the Key to Peak Performance in Sports and in Life," appeared in the August 3, 1992, issue of the same magazine. Brian Hatfield of the University of Maryland reported that at moments of peak performance, the brain's left side, the analytic side, erupts in a burst of relaxing alpha waves, indicative of a relaxed, trancelike state. This allows the right side of the brain, which controls spatial relations and pattern recognition, to control the body.

OK, what do these studies have to do with kids playing basketball? They help us understand and correct inconsistencies. Research suggests several steps you can take to create or strive for the conditions optimal to peak performance.

Repetition, Repetition, Repetition

One step we already take, and have for years, is repetition. The best way to produce a controlled response to game-day excitement is constant repetition during practice. Much of this book deals with the need to repeatedly practice dribbling and shooting, including adherence to proper form. This is so the game responses become automatic, and can occur even if the player is under stress or is too excited.

Follow a Game-Day Pattern

Both studies also suggest that a ritual-like approach to game day is conducive to the relaxed state of mind needed. A regular pattern of eating, exercise, dressing and pregame discussion is highly recommended. Try to avoid any surprises or deviations. The preset mental routine should apply right up to the opening buzzer.

Prepare the Mind

Tell kids that they need to *prepare the mind as well as the body if they are to reach their best potential*. Encourage them to run through a checklist of form (e.g., hands up, eye on the ball, stay low, follow through with the gooseneck). Tell them to mentally picture the play, imagine themselves with great form stealing the ball and driving to the hoop. This stuff works! It is well accepted at the highest levels of sport.

Sports psychologists have anticipated current research findings in their long-time support of mental imaging of athletic routines. Olympic athletes have been tracing their steps mentally for years. Now we have clear scientific bases for this approach.

Don't Let the Adrenalin Build Up Too Early

Sapolsky notes that premature arousal of adrenalin hours before the game can result in the level in the blood dropping after a few hours, even to a point below normal at game time. This will lead to subpar performance and is another reason to have relaxed, stable pregame routines. Many coaches now employ Zen-type meditations in the training programs, providing athletes with methods to evoke relaxed states of mind at will.

Use These Techniques At All Levels

Control techniques are useful at all levels of play. They are perhaps most needed at the youngest levels where kids cannot control the anxieties of competition. Relaxed game day rituals, mental imaging, affirmations of self-esteem, mental checklists (such as contained throughout this book), are techniques that can be repeatedly practiced.

Get an Edge

Many coaches have some concept they use to focus players on achieving peak performance. I always told my players to try to *get an edge* over their opponent. We talked about how evenly matched most good teams usually are, and that the winner would be the team who got some kind of edge over the opponent.

This concept helped me to get kids to accept, for instance, the idea of improving their mental approach—as one way to get an edge. I would tell kids to double the number of pushups they could do, since the other kids on other teams probably weren't doing it, and so they would get a bit stronger than them.

ON PARENTS

As you know, parents can be a great help in youth sports; however, *interfering parents* can be a major problem for coaches. This is especially true in basketball because parents are usually right on top of the team, so their complaining is more visible.

I have no problem with parents who, after the game, want to talk to the coach and find out whether there is some problem they need to be aware of. But often they are argumentative, and sometimes downright insulting.

Of course, you don't need to take any gas from a pain in the neck. But before you get too defensive, think about what's going on.

Parents Feel for Their Kids

Most parents literally die a little bit when they see their child going through a bad time. Maybe she is not playing much, having self-doubts, and acting out at home or school because of it. Parents feel the pain along with their kids—it's tough for a kid, or anyone, to find out she's not good enough.

Offer Suggestions

Hear parents out! Give them some ideas to help understand what the problem is, and perhaps you can focus them on things they can do to help at home. Tell them you are "on" the kid because you think he can do better, and you are trying to arouse his potential. Maybe, in return, you can get some insight into what is troubling the child. Maybe, just maybe, you are dead wrong; and you need to give the kid another look. Tell the parents you will do that. I've seen kids sit on the bench as a sub for half a season, suddenly come alive, and wind up as starters.

Be Understanding

Most of all, keep in mind that *she's their kid!* They may feel a bit threatened by your control over their child. As a parent, I have had uneasy feelings about coaches: It's quite natural. A little patience on your part can defuse some strong emotions. You can turn a potential feud into something that helps the child and, ultimately, the team. Try it.

Don't Tolerate Abuse

A major problem is the parent who abuses his child during a game. He scorns his son or daughter for missing a shot or bad defense. It's the worst thing in sports to see. You do not have to put up with this! Talk to the parent and ask him to keep quiet. If he doesn't, remove him from the gym. While I was coaching baseball, one parent threatened me with removing his son as well. My response was merely that I hoped he wouldn't, but that not playing was probably better than what was going on and that it would not continue under my watch! The parent stayed home; the kid played.

Empower Parents

Frankly, as noted earlier, I rarely had problems with parents. When you achieve a certain level of team spirit, it becomes infectious and negativity gets left behind. I always sought to empower parents, get them involved with the team in some manner: as coaches, as drill monitors, in charge of water breaks, in charge of fund drives, in charge of uniforms, on phone trees. Delegate as much as possible, and you'll bring parents into the team dynamic.

Chapter seven points out ways parents can help keep more activity going on in practice. They can rebound for shooting practice, provide light dummy defense, coach their kids at home. Push gently to get them involved: Don't push too hard.

Some Notes for Parents

Parents would be wise to follow these guidelines:

Evaluate Your Child's Potential and Desire, and Be Honest

If he is a beginner, the first objective is to learn the game fundamentals. Go over terminology and concepts. Take him to a high school, college or pro game. Sign him up for a clinic. Start by promoting dribbling, lay-ups and short jump shots.

As Your Child Improves, Begin to Apply Mild Pressure During Your Practice Sessions

Don't dominate your child. (I used to defend against my sons initially without using my hands.) Increase pressure as she can take it, challenge her. Begin to introduce other concepts—give and go, pick and roll, screening, stealing the ball, rebounding. As short jumpers are mastered, move farther out. Practice foul shots.

As Your Child Becomes a Decent Player, You Can Help by Concentrating on Specific Skills

If he's tall, give him low post practice while you defend, again, only aggressively enough to make it a challenge. Forwards should shoot from the corners and wing, and practice baseline drives. Guards needs to practice speed dribbling, so apply open-court defensive pressure. Practice snappy passing and outside shooting from above the high post. Set goals to improve free throw percentage. If he can only make 3 out of 20, work to get it to 5, 7, 10 and 15.

Encourage Your Daughter to Play if She Wants to Play

Basketball is popular for both boys and girls, and the girls' teams are growing rapidly. It seems to me when viewing girls' games that girls don't spend as much time shooting as boys do. Their shot percentages are much lower. If your daughter is interested in playing, concentrate on jump shots—she can be a star very quickly.

The menstrual cycle should not be a great problem. Explain to your daughter the importance of exercise in building strength and reducing menstrual discomfort. Your daughter will know if she feels up to practicing or playing. If she feels weak or is uncomfortable from cramps, a note to the coach should excuse her. Most coaches will be understanding. Your daughter should wear an athletic bra to protect muscle tone.

How Can You Get Your Child Interested in Sports?

The most important thing is to avoid the negative stuff, as we have repeated often in this book. If your child is afraid of competition, fearful of being embarrassed or tired of your impatience (if you are yelling at her, and getting annoyed or frustrated), she will never be interested.

Tell her there is an athlete inside somewhere, and you are going to work with her to develop it. Communicate. Discuss the things in this book—talk basketball, go to a pro game or to a local high school game. Watch some on TV, work with your child in trying to collect a whole series of basketball cards. If you go out and coach her and she gets better, you won't have to worry about interest.

Many afternoons I got home from work and my sons were on the stoop with a basketball. The court was across the street. "Hey Dad, you ready to play?" Interest? I can't turn it off. We became buddies through sports. You work closely with your child on something like this, and she will not only be interested in basketball, she'll become interested in you. How can you lose?

Parental Behavior at Games

I'm not going to tell you to just sit there and be quiet. I'm not going to tell you to reduce your energy by one iota. But if you read this book carefully, you'll know how to act at games.

First, don't pressure your child, or anyone else's. Second, say intelligent, helpful things like "get the ball," "make it happen," "pressure," "in their faces,"—things that will help him remember the basics. Study the list of motivational phrases for encouraging words to call out. Be positive.

At games, get to know the other parents. It's really a beautiful thing when a team becomes one big family. Most of mine have been that way, because I promote it as a high priority. It makes everything more loose, more relaxed, and that's better for the kids. It can also lead to some rewarding friendships and to a deeper feeling of communication, and that's icing on the cake. In addition, you might get another parent more interested in helping his or her son, and that's super. Finally, suggest they read this book.

How to Deal With the Coach

I hope you will have read this book and practiced with your child for a year before you even meet your child's first coach. Then you can offer your help as an assistant, or even sign up for the top job. At six- to eight-years-old, there is not much skill on the court to worry about, and it is a good starting place for inexperienced coaches.

Get Involved

I suggest you find some way to get involved. When the coach calls, offer whatever help you can give. If your job takes up your weekdays, offer to help on weekends. Many coaches will be happy for it. Some don't want help, so there's not much you can do; but you can still work with your child at home.

Some parents just like to sit and watch practice. I don't mind; most coaches won't either. Besides, it will help you become aware of areas where your child can use improvement.

Fairness Is a Two-Way Street

If your child is playing the minimum, but only the minimum, be fair before you approach the coach. Usually, coaches are out to win, and they do play the best players. Just work a little harder, and your child may improve enough to play more.

If the coach is being unfair, talk to him about it. It is a difficult thing for all involved, so please be sure it's not just your ego complaining.

And for goodness sakes, try to keep your child out of the debate. He doesn't need the negative images involved. Don't get mad. The coach could take it out on your child. But don't duck it either. A few questions to the coach, nicely stated, will help, such as, "What can Johnny do to get more playing time?"

If the coach is a negative person, and you will probably get one for your child at some point, you may need to let the local board know about it. Bad coaches need to be weeded out. They can do a lot of damage.

Chapter Nine

YOUR PLAYERS' HEALTH

VISION

The following will be the most important section in this book for some of your players, maybe for your own child. It reveals what may be the best kept secret in basketball and perhaps in all of sports. It's about vision, eyesight: how critical it is and how to improve it.

As I look back on my nearly two decades of coaching sports, I'm reminded of the many young players who came to the game full of hope and excitement but who just never made it. Others did well enough but, inexplicably, they continually performed below the level I expected for them. Like all kids, they dreamed of those game-winning jump shots or steals. They just never seemed to get it done.

Some of these kids were good athletes. They knew they could do better, knew they had it in them, but only could put up average numbers. Some had a miserable season or two and never came back to the game.

Surely, for many it just wasn't there. Their gifts of life were elsewhere, in the laboratory, with music, or in other skills, just not in basketball. That's life! But I have become convinced that for many a substantial part of the problem was merely in their inability to see clearly enough to shoot with precision, catch a short quick pass or see the whole floor of play.

I'm not describing major differences in eyesight in this chapter. Just a small subtle difference in visual acuity is enough to lead to enormous differences in how well one can catch, pass, dribble or shoot basketballs.

This fact is not lost on professional players. Vision therapy is a rapidly growing staple of the off-season preparation of major league players. The sports literature reports that many other sports such as golf, tennis, hockey and baseball are including emphasis on visual acuity in training routines. This eye training consists of a series of vision tests, exercises for the fourteen eye muscles and follow-up workouts designed to improve concentration, visual focus, depth perception and hand-eye coordination.

In an astonishing book, *20/20 Is Not Enough*, Arthur S. Seiderman and Steven E. Marcus revealed new and effective ways to dramatically improve vision. They claimed that 70 percent of Americans have less than adequate vision. Moreover, vision is not fully developed until age ten or eleven. Intensive reading in school, watching television, and working at computer terminals all further reduce visual acuity. So, is it surprising that so many ten-year-olds have difficulty hitting the front of the rim from 15 feet away? What is really frustrating is that the book suggests that most visual disorders go undiagnosed and could easily be treated.

The good news is that vision can be improved. Even if your child has 20/20 vision, this does not mean he cannot improve other aspects of vision such as depth perception, the ability to track clearly a fast-moving object and hand-eye coordination. The difference with only a small amount of therapy can be enormous.

It is not the objective of this book to give medical advice or to go in depth on the biology of the eye itself. The book I mentioned above is available in bookstores or libraries (Knopf, 1989). Other superb books are: *Healthy Eyes, Better Vision* by Jeffrey Anshel (Body Press, 1990); and *Your Eyes!* by Thomas L. D'Alonzo (Avanti Publishing, 1991).

Suffice it to say here that the eyes are like binoculars, and when they don't work well together they get out of focus, resulting in difficulty in seeing things that are close (hyperopia or farsightedness), difficulty in seeing things far away (myopia or nearsightedness), difficulty judging depth or speed of an approaching object, or other ailments.

I advise you to see an eye doctor and have your child's eyes tested. If one of your players seems to have some difficulty seeing the ball, suggest it to the parents. Tell them to read this book, so they can consider whether it would be useful to engage in vision therapy even if there is a more obvious eye disorder.

Vision therapy has advanced far enough that some exercises can safely be done at home. I'll list a few that appear more commonly in the literature and that apply to the skills needed in basketball. Again, the best practice is to first seek a doctor's advice.

Vision Therapy Drills

1. Brock string. Tie a 4-foot string, with a large knot or black tape marking the center and a point several inches from each end, to an object at eye level while seated. Stretch the line taut and hold against the nose. Looking at the center spot will reveal an X pattern. (See Figure 9-1.) The far spot will reveal an A pattern, and the near spot a V pattern. Practice shifting the gaze from spot to spot until it feels smooth and easy to do. Eventually you can shorten the string. Do this for several minutes each

FIGURE 9-1

VISION THERAPY DRILLS

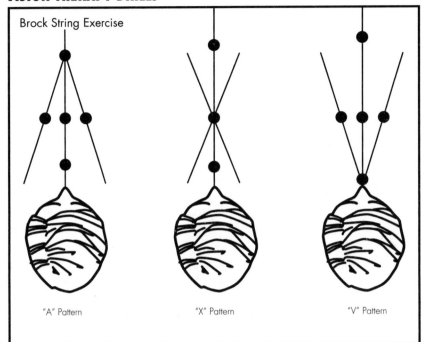

Brock String Exercise

"A" Pattern   "X" Pattern   "V" Pattern

The *brock string vision therapy drill* improves focusing and depth perception. See the text for a detailed explanation of the drill.

day. It will improve focusing and depth perception. This drill can be done at home or at practice. (Check with parents first!)

2. Marsden ball. Get a rubber ball about 4 inches in diameter. Suspend it from overhead to about eye level while seated. Write letters and numbers all over the ball in ink. (They should be clear, dark letters on a light-colored ball.) Cover one eye and tap the ball lightly. Try to call out a letter you see and quickly touch it with your finger. Do each eye for a few minutes. (See Figure 9-2.) This improves eye-hand coordination and the ability to track a moving object. If the ball can be affixed securely enough, use a broom handle to bounce it off a wall. Try to maintain a fluid and continuous pace. Use a smaller ball to make it tougher. With parental consent, the Marsden ball drill can be done at practice. Have one player hold the string for another.

3. Fixation drill. Hang a ring from a string to eye level while standing. Stand a step away with a long pencil. Cover the left eye, step toward the

ring with the right foot and, holding the pencil in the right hand, try to put the pencil through the ring without touching it. After a few minutes switch eyes, use the left hand, and step with the left foot. After mastering this drill, try it with a moving target. This drill improves hand-eye coordination. (See Figure 9-2.)

4. Rotations. Place a marble in a pie tin or frying pan held about 15 to 18 inches from the eyes. Holding the head still, rotate the marble and try to follow it for a few minutes. Change direction for another two minutes. This improves tracking ability. (See Figure 9-2.)

5. Accommodation drill. Doctors use a device called an Accomotrac, based on biofeedback theory, to improve focusing problems, particularly nearsightedness. An exercise you can do is to sit with a newspaper with normal-sized print at just below eye level, as close as possible to the eye, then place another newspaper with large headlines 15 to 20 feet away. Cover one eye. Shift focus back and forth from one to the other. This can be done with any nearby small object and any distant object.

6. Convergence drills. Place this book on a desk with Figure 9-3 at normal reading distance. Hold a pencil between the two sets of circles and slowly move the pencil point toward your eyes. At a point about 6 inches from your eyes, a third circle will appear between the other two. The outer circle should appear closer than the inner one. When it seems clear, shift the eyes to something else and bring them back again to the pencil tip. Do this until the focus remains smooth and clear upon the middle figure. Do it ten times.

Another convergence drill is to hold the circles up at reading distance but just below eye level. Sit several feet from a wall. Focus on the wall, and the third circle should again appear. This time the small inner circle should appear closer. Close eyes and reopen to the pencil point. Do this several times until the focus stays smooth and clear. After this is mastered, the pencil can be dispensed with, and the distance of the figures can be made a bit closer. You can also draw the figures on separate cards and separate them more (just a bit, don't strain). Always try to get to a clear focus on the center set of circles.

Teach these drills to your players at practice. Tell them to do them at home. Some can be done on the court by subs during scrimmages or just before practice. Talk to parents first. Tell parents to get this book and read this section. Your team's vision will improve. Shooting, passing and receiving will improve. Hopefully, some of those kids who otherwise wouldn't make it will have some fun with this great game!

FIGURE 9-2

VISION THERAPY DRILLS

To improve eye-hand coordination and eye tracking, players should perfrom the *marsden ball drill*. It is described in detail in the text.

Another good eye-hand coordination exercise is the *fixation drill*. See the text for a detailed explanation.

Rotations improve eye tracking and can be done at home or on the practice court.

The *convergence drill* practices the quickness and clarity with which the eyes can change focus on objects at varying distances. It also improves depth perception. This drill is explained further in the text.

One final thought. Do you know which of your eyes is the dominant one? Make a circle with your thumb and index finger, and extend your arm out at eye level. Fix your sight on a small object and close one eye,

FIGURE 9-3
CONVERGENCE DRILLS

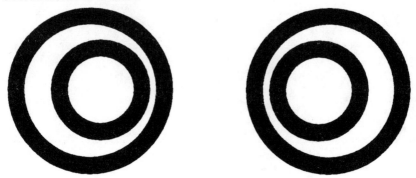

Use these circles when practicing the *convergence drill.*

then open it and close the other. The dominant eye is the one for which the object does not move! Shooters should turn their heads a bit so the dominant eye looks more directly at the hoop.

CONDITIONING

I rarely recommend weight training for youth sports, and I certainly don't do so for basketball. I'll discuss this more later in this section. A good calisthenic program is adequate, and a list of exercises was given in chapter seven. Pushups on the fingertips are the best exercise since forearm and wrist strength is important in basketball. Tell your players to do fifty to one hundred per day. Chin-ups, as many as the player can do, are also quite helpful. Wrist, forearm and shoulder strength are crucial, and any help that you can give here will be immediately and quite noticeably rewarded on the court. I got my son a set of chest expanders, with springs attached to handles, and he used to do them while watching cartoons. The wrist machine mentioned in chapter seven is great for home or practice. I always had one in my duffle bag, and the kids used it after shooting practice. Rowing exercises are also very good to increase strength and stamina.

After the arms and upper body come the legs. Wind sprints are the best leg exercise. Partial squats, halfway bending the knee with some extra weight added, are quite good. Don't bend all the way. The longstanding tradition of running up stairs is excellent.

Muscles are like bubble gum. If you stretch gum quickly it tears or snaps, but if you stretch it slowly it expands nicely. Stretching before practice and before games will help prevent muscles from tearing or snapping. No practice of any kind should begin without some slow jogging, some jumping jacks (for the ankles), and some general stretching (for the upper thigh, trunk and neck). Running sideways and backward or any agility exercises are quite good also.

As noted, I generally believe that weight training should be avoided by grade-school level players and not started until mid-high-school years. Part of the reason is intuitive: A child's body is growing rapidly until then. I am also aware of some studies done in the 1970s that demonstrated that grade-school kids do not gain strength from weight lifting due to lack of male hormones. These studies also suggested that there was significant risk of injury to kids' growth plates, which are the ends of the long bones that account for growth.

A careful study of 354 high-school football players by Dr. William Risser of the University of Texas Medical School found that weight lifting can cause severe musculoskeletal injuries, usually muscle strains and often in the lower back—7.1 percent of the players reported injury. Injuries occurred when free weights were used in major lifts such as the clean and jerk, the snatch, the squat lift, the dead lift, the power clean and in the bench, incline and overhead presses. Most injuries occurred in the home and were related to poor technique and form, lack of warm-up, and lack of a spotter to assist.

However, I must report that more recent research suggests a different point of view from my own. In the November 1990 issue of *Pediatrics* (Vol. 86, No.5), the American Academy of Pediatrics Committee on Sports Medicine said, "Recent research has shown that short-term programs in which prepubescent [grade school] athletes are trained and supervised by knowledgeable adults can increase strength without significant injury risk." The statement went on to say: "Interscholastic athletic programs in secondary schools are increasingly emphasizing strength training as a conditioning method for participants in male and female sports. The major lifts are often used . . . Strength training in adolescence occasionally produces significant musculoskeletal injury . . . especially during use of the major lifts. Safety requires careful planning of several aspects of a program. This includes devising a program for the intensity, duration, frequency, and rate of progression of weight use, as well as selection of sport-specific exercises appropriate for the physical maturity of the individual. Proper supervision should be provided during training sessions." The committee also addressed the issue of when kids should be allowed to lift maximal amounts of weight, that is, the greatest amount of weight they can successfully lift. They concluded that this should be avoided until kids have passed their period of maximal velocity of height growth. Young people reach that stage *on average* at age fifteen, but the committee also notes that there is "much individual variation." Consequently, based on the contents of this article, the American Academy of Pediatrics recommends that each child's stage of physical maturity be assessed by medical personnel and that the adults planning strength training programs be qualified to develop programs appropriate for varying stages of maturity.

Another good article, "Strength Training in Children and Adolescents" (*Pediatric Clinics of North America*, October 1990), was written by Dr. David Webb at the Center for Sportsmedicine, Saint Francis Memorial Hospital, San Francisco, California. He found that most injuries occurred in the home and were unsupervised and that there is not an inordinate risk of injury in weight training if it's properly done. He also reported that strength training can help kids excel in sports and that it can actually *reduce* the incidence of muscle or tendon injuries in sports.

What does this all mean? Knowledgeable trainers can help young athletes gain strength at all levels of play, and weight training will help them do so. Since most kids are urged to do it, those who don't will be at a disadvantage. However, any program should avoid maximal weight lifts until the mid-high-school years.

Be careful; injury can still occur no matter what. Let's face it. Anyone who has ever lifted weights knows that even if you follow a good program, kids have a powerful urge to finish up with some heavy weights to see how much they can lift. If unsupervised, they will go for the max at some point. This is one of the main reasons I frown on the idea. I also resent the idea that we should heighten the competitive pressure of athletics in grade school by creating a need to strength train to "keep up." But the reality is that at the high school level, players will need to do weights if they are to be competitive. As a parent you must ensure that they are supervised and that they follow a sound program. A 7 percent injury rate for unsupervised training is quite high, so parents must assert controls on this matter.

A player who undertakes a weight training program, as advised above, should have the supervision and advice of a knowledgeable trainer. Parents should ask their doctor if any pre-existing health conditions can be aggravated by such training. High blood pressure is one condition that doesn't mix with weights. Any pain should be reported to the trainer. Warm-up and stretching exercises should be done before lifting. Lifting maximal weights or engaging in *ballistic* sudden jerking exercises such as clean and jerk should not be done. Kids should generally use weights that can be done in sets of fifteen repetitions. They should not lift every day, but every other day at the most. All major muscle groups should get some attention to keep development balanced.

In the weight room, basketball players should emphasize legs (upper and lower) and upper body (shoulders, arms and wrists). I already mentioned partial squats. Do hamstring curls, too. A good calf exercise is to sit on a chair with weight on the top of the thighs and toes on a block of wood. Raise the weight with the toes. Exercises with dumbbells for shoulder, wrist and forearm are great, especially for rebounding. Bench presses will help—if the bench inclines it's better. Do wrist curls also. Let the trainer explain how to do these and other exercises needed for a balanced program.

INJURIES

Is there a trainer or someone qualified in first aid at practice? This is *very* important during early days of practice. Most leagues require coaches to obtain licenses that expose them to first aid techniques, but is there someone who really knows what to do? If not, remember that parents can take a course and become quite knowledgeable. Perhaps you can get a parent to volunteer as a trainer.

I watched a practice game once in which a kid twisted his knee. The coach was shorthanded for players and seemed more concerned about getting the kid back into the game than worrying about the extent of any injury. A few minutes later the kid was back in the action. After a while I noticed he was limping a bit. The coach never looked at him! I told the coach, and the player was removed. As a parent, it pays to attend a few practices to see how sensitive the coach is to injury. A good rule is that a player who complains of any injury to any joint cannot play for at least ten minutes to see if pain or swelling is still present.

No matter how well conditioned a team is, injuries can occur anytime. A common injury is a groin strain, usually caused by sprinting down the court without warming up. Blisters, nosebleeds, finger jams, floor burns, shin splints and athlete's foot are the most common basketball injuries. Shin splints is a painful soreness in the shins which arises from playing on different surfaces (indoor and outdoor) or from not warming up. Make sure your players wear socks covering the shins to keep them warm. Kids today like to push the socks down, and it's not good for them. Athlete's foot is a fungus that thrives in damp, warm environments. There are good antiseptic powders for this. Players should thoroughly dry their feet after practice and frequently change socks. Sprained or strained wrists and forearms, sprained ankles and bruises also occur. Thankfully, broken bones are rare, but not rare enough. Most youth basketball teams don't have trained first-aid people, and they should. I went through the program for my son's team, and it was quite good.

Abrasions, or floor burns, often occur on the sides of the legs and elbows, from sliding on the gym floor. These are the most likely cuts to get infected. Wash the wound as soon as possible, with soap if it is handy. Apply a dressing when you can—the sooner the better. Just put some antiseptic on it. If it gets red, pussy or red tracks appear, see a physician.

Lacerations are deeper wounds. Unless bleeding is severe, wash the wound and apply direct pressure with a bandage to stop the bleeding. If the wound is severe or deep, seek first aid. Keep applying pressure, and secure the dressing with a bandage (you can tie the knot right over the wound to reinforce the pressure). Immediately elevate the wound higher than the heart to help slow the bleeding. If the bandage over the wound gets blood-soaked, don't remove it—just apply a new dressing right over it. If the child has lost a lot of blood, you'll need to treat for shock. Keep the player warm with blankets and call for help. If a laceration is major, a butterfly bandage will hold the skin together. Consult a physician immediately for stitches.

Contusions and bruises occur frequently. Apply ice quickly after taking care of any abrasions or lacerations. Ice arrests internal bleeding and prevents or lessens swelling. Ice is the best first aid available for nearly any swelling from bruises or sprains. Apply it very quickly, within minutes, and much internal damage will be spared. Do not move the child, especially if he is down due to a hard collision. He could have a spinal injury, and the slightest movement by an untrained person could do some serious damage.

Sprained ankles, knees or wrists should be immobilized. Apply an ice pack immediately. Act as if there is a fracture until you're sure there is no fracture. Call the ambulance if there is any question in your mind. Get an x-ray to see if there is a break or other damage.

If there is a fracture, immobilize the child completely when possible. There should be no movement at all. Comfort her, get her warm with coats or blankets and get medical help. Do not allow your child to be moved or cared for by anyone who is not medically trained. If she is in the middle of the court during a championship game, the game can wait! Insist on this. Permanent damage can result from aggravating a break.

If a child ever falls to the ground unconscious, see if anyone present has been trained in first aid. The first move, once it is clear that the child will not respond, is to check for the vital signs: airway, breathing and circulation, the ABCs of first aid. Send for an ambulance and let a trained person administer rescue breathing or CPR (cardiopulmonary resuscitation) as necessary. Try to stay calm and let the first-aiders do their job. In all my years of coaching four sports and playing even more, I've never seen CPR needed. I hope that you won't either.

Finally, heat exhaustion can occur during practices or games, particularly late in the game. The body gets clammy and pale. Remove the child from the game, apply cool towels and elevate the feet. If the body temperature is very high and pupils are constricted, you should suspect heat stroke. Call an ambulance and cool him down fast. Treat for shock.

Knee injuries are tough. Often the injury will require some sort of arthroscopic surgery to mend cartilage. Modern procedures are quite advanced and simple. Have the child see a knowledgeable sports doctor. Your high school athletic director will know one. Tell your child to play the game safely. Aggressiveness is OK, but players should never intentionally hurt someone. Hope that other parents do the same. I play various sports frequently, and there are often one or two guys who take chances with the health of others. Don't encourage your child to grow up to be like them.

When an injury occurs, insist on rest. I've seen many kids rush back from a sprained ankle, only to have the injury plague them through the years. Don't let it happen! And make sure that your child wears an ankle brace from then on. There are excellent ankle braces on the market today. Get one. The point is that injuries need time to heal right. If you give them that time, the future can have many years of sports for your child. If you don't, it could be over already.

Serious Injuries

Catastrophic spine or brain injuries among any athletes, especially basketball players, are rare, yet they happen. There are cases, for example, where kids hit a wall or obstruction with the head. This is obviously a most unpleasant subject, but it is important that you understand some detail. Many deadly injuries of the brain or paralyzing injuries of the spine are caused by earlier blows, sometimes one that occurred a week or more earlier, and a concerned and informed parent can step in and avoid it. A player can receive a concussion, never black out, and that brain swelling can then become lethal days later, triggered by a relatively minor blow.

The point is that *any* level of confusion or headache brought on by a blow to the head should receive *immediate* medical attention. I don't care if it's a championship game—get the player out of the game! The Colorado

Medical Society recommends that players who sustain a severe blow to the head be removed for at least 20 minutes and not be allowed to return to the game if any confusion or amnesia persists during that time. A player who loses consciousness should go straight to the hospital.

THE CARBOHYDRATE DIET

Parents can do only so much to improve their child's athletic ability, but they can do a great deal to maintain his or her good health. All sports require a great deal of energy, and a healthy body goes a long way toward better performance on the court and avoiding injury.

Obviously, a balanced diet is essential. There are many books on diet, and your doctor or school nurse can also advise on the elements of good diet. Good nutrition helps develop strength, endurance and concentration. A good diet balances proteins, carbohydrates and fats. An athlete in training needs mainly complex carbohydrates, about 70 percent of the total diet, with fats (10 percent) and proteins (20 percent) splitting the remainder. Popular today is the food guide pyramid. (See Figure 9-4.) Complex carbohydrates dominate the base grouping, reflecting the greater doses of breads, cereal, rice and pasta that are recommended. Vegetables and fruits take up the next level, calling for a few daily servings each. The dairy group and the meat, fish and poultry group are next, with fats last.

Early in the season, an evening meal high in carbohydrates helps maintain energy the next day. Pasta is the best meal for this. A banana each day during this early period helps prevent potassium depletion. Potassium facilitates the process of muscular contraction. Complex carbohydrates are the primary source of fuel and energy for the athlete. They are broken down into glucose, the body's main source of energy. What is not needed is stored for future use. Avoid simple carbohydrates such as sugar and honey. The adage that a candy bar just before a game gives an energy boost is misleading since simple carbohydrates cause unstable supplies of glucose. (Ever notice how tired you feel after a sweets overload?) Good sources of complex carbohydrates are corn on the cob, wild rice, brown rice, whole wheat and whole rye.

A Typical High-Carbohydrate Diet

Breakfast
- 8 oz. orange juice or a grapefruit or 8 oz. apple juice
- Bowl of shredded wheat (low-fat milk) or oatmeal or cream of farina
- (a) Bacon and two eggs or (b) pancakes and butter

FIGURE 9-4
FOOD GUIDE PYRAMID

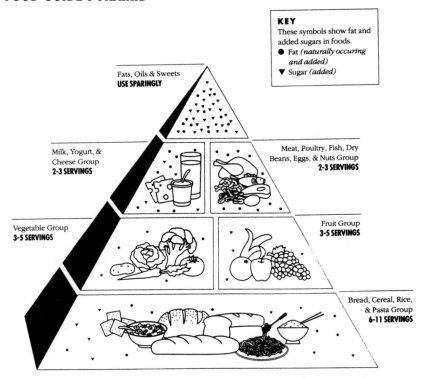

The pyramid is an outline of what to eat each day. It's not a rigid prescription, but a general guide that lets you choose a healthful diet that's right for you. The Pyramid calls for eating a variety of foods to get the nutrients you need and at the same time the right amount of calories to maintain a healthy weight.

The food guide pyramid will help your players plan their daily food intake.

- Several slices of whole wheat toast and butter
- Daily vitamin, adult dosage
- 10 oz. water

Lunch
- 1 bowl of soup: chicken, clam chowder or vegetable
- 2 pieces broiled chicken or 6 oz. broiled fish
- Green salad with oil and vinegar
- Cooked rice or a potato (no french fries)
- 2 slices of enriched bread
- 12 to 16 oz. milk
- 10 oz. water

Dinner
- 1 bowl of soup: cream of mushroom, cream of potato or vegetable
- Linguine with tomato or clam sauce
- Baked potato
- Cooked vegetable: corn, broccoli, peas or beans
- Beverage of choice
- 10 oz. water

Desserts or Snacks
- Bananas, apples, raisins, strawberries or melons
- 10 oz. water

Most teams allow water breaks, so make sure parents know to get their child a water bottle. Midpractice is not a good time to load up on water, so tell the kids to limit themselves to a cup at each break. Kids need a couple of quarts a day, more if it's hot and they are playing outside. Drinking plenty of water is a good habit, so be sure they know to drink some at each meal. It is also important to drink plenty of fluids before, during and after practices. Dehydration reduces performance and can lead to serious medical problems.

Alcohol, tobacco and drugs have effects we are all too aware of. What young players may not think about enough is that these substances substantially reduce their playing performance, and reduced performance can put a child out of the running for a starting position, or even for making the team. Be sure to discuss this practical concern.

Sufficient sleep is also a concern. If your son or daughter starts the season with hard sessions of practice, you won't have to worry too much at first, since your child will come right home and hit the pillow. However, into the season, particularly at high school levels, a player may try to burn the candle at both ends. Again, I find that kids relate better when they consider practical consequences of their actions. Lack of sufficient rest diminishes performance. Diminished performance costs playing time.

Chapter Ten

COACH'S AND PARENT'S CHECKLIST

Okay, now it's time to get out to the basketball court with your child or team. I find it useful when I coach to have a checklist of things to look for or to say as I work with my kids. A glance at the checklist below is a reminder. Repetition of key phrases helps your child concentrate on basics.

DRIBBLING
The best confidence-builder for a beginner.
- ☐ Keep the ball out on the fingers.
- ☐ Receive the ball, withdraw the hand, cradle it and pump back out.
- ☐ Arm and body move with the rhythm of the ball.
- ☐ Develop both hands.
- ☐ Head up, eyes front.
- ☐ Keep ball and body low in traffic.
- ☐ Shield ball with the body.
- ☐ Practice head, shoulder, ball, body, pass and shot fakes.
- ☐ Use the pivot freely.

PASSING
- ☐ Quick, snappy passes are critical to good team play.
- ☐ Know where teammates are.
- ☐ Use pivot to buy time.
- ☐ Use two hands.
- ☐ Spread fingers and rotate fingertips up and into chest area.
- ☐ Step toward the receiver.
- ☐ Snap wrists and fingers outward.
- ☐ Don't broadcast the pass.
- ☐ Lead the receiver. Pass to open space.
- ☐ Pass to the receiver's chest or outstretched hand.
- ☐ Pass to the side of receiver opposite the defender.

☐ Overhead pass from a rebound, or to get ball over defender.
☐ Baseball style for long passes.

RECEIVING PASSES
☐ Always know where the ball is.
☐ Don't turn your back to ball handler.
☐ Always want and anticipate a pass.
☐ Move to the pass.
☐ Give a target hand.
☐ Soft hands.
☐ Keep the eyes on the ball.

SHOOTING
The essence of basketball.
☐ Shoot within your range.
☐ Triple-threat balance.
☐ Jab step to get free.
☐ Jump straight, off both feet.
☐ Shots start in and come from the legs.
☐ Cradle high.
☐ Shoulders and head square.
☐ Point shooting elbow to the hoop.
☐ Flick wrist, 30° reverse spin, gooseneck finish.
☐ Shoot with only one hand, other hand cradles only.
☐ Achieve reasonable arc.
☐ Soft hands.
☐ Follow the shot.
☐ Always look for open man underneath.
☐ Aim to sit ball on point of hoop closest to you.
☐ Keep options open.
☐ If ball consistently hits back of rim, use more wrist and less forearm.

Lay-ups are great confidence builders.
☐ Claim the lane.
☐ Submarine.
☐ Take two big steps.
☐ Lift knee on shooting hand side.
☐ Lay ball up softly.
☐ Rotate landing.

Foul shots.

- ☐ Must be constantly practiced.
- ☐ Point shooting-side foot at hoop.
- ☐ Be comfortable.
- ☐ Start low.
- ☐ Cradle, raise high, flick and gooseneck.
- ☐ Point elbow at hoop.
- ☐ Square head and shoulders.
- ☐ Extend body fully, up on toes, and hold extension.
- ☐ Post up underneath, fake to one side, and drop step the other way.
- ☐ Avoid dribbling underneath.

OFFENSE

- ☐ Look for high percentage shot, in shooter's range, without undue defensive pressure.
- ☐ Look for post man.
- ☐ Attack from wing.
- ☐ Pick and roll.
- ☐ Give and go.
- ☐ Don't be too quick to dribble.
- ☐ Jab and rocker steps.
- ☐ Shoot when open inside of 12 feet.
- ☐ Run the offense.
- ☐ Cut and flash the lane.

DEFENSE

- ☐ Get back on defense quickly.
- ☐ Pressure.
- ☐ Confuse the ball handler.
- ☐ Keep the ball wide, away from the lane.
- ☐ Avoid bad fouls, especially underneath.
- ☐ Deny to plays underneath.
- ☐ Fight through or sink behind screen.
- ☐ Switch and slow down pick and roll until help arrives.
- ☐ Trap when possible.
- ☐ Triple-threat.
- ☐ Look for steals—track ball with ball-side hand.
- ☐ Rebound, box out, catch with two hands.

GLOSSARY

Airball: An outside shot that misses the hoop, backboard, everything. At college games, fans will razz a player who has shot an airball every time he gets his hands on the ball thereafter.

Arc: The path of a shot ball. A low arc is called a brick, an overly high arc, a rainmaker. Ordinarily, an arc should be about 15-feet from the floor on a 15-foot jump shot.

Backboard: The rectangular or semicircular fan-shaped surface on which the basket is mounted, used for bank shots. It is also called the glass, if so constructed. In outside lots, it's usually made of wood or metal. The backboard has been called a bankboard or a bangboard.

Backcourt: The half of the court where the ball isn't in play. In the early days, some players stayed back on defense all the time, by rule, and were called backcourt players. Now the term is used to described the area itself, and the offense can't take the ball into the backcourt area once they completely cross the mid-court line (also called the backcourt line).

Ball: Usually leather, the circumference must be 29½ to 30 inches for boys and an inch less for girls. Weight is 20 to 22 ounces for boys, 2 ounces less for girls. It should be inflated to a pressure so that it will bounce to a height of 49 to 54 inches at the top when dropped from more than 6 feet.

Bank Shot: The ball hits the backboard before it goes in. Sometimes it's just a lucky shot, although the shooter will smile as though he intended to bank it.

Baseline: The end-line boundary at each end of the court, under the hoop. A baseline drive is very effective if you can get by the defender. The baseline, however, is out of bounds.

Basket: The 18-inch circumference hoop that players shoot at. Also known as a bucket. When the ball goes through, it is a field goal and one, two or three points are awarded.

Block: To reject or repel a shot ball before it hits the top of its arc. Usually, it is just called a rejection.

Box-out: A defensive move using the back of the body to screen a player from getting a rebound.

Center: Usually the tallest player on the team. He or she plays underneath, in the lane, where the action is.

Charge: A player control foul committed by a driving offensive player hitting a stationary defender who has established his position. The defense gets possession.

Circle: An offensive move without the ball in which the player circles his defender to turn and confuse him and then breaks free for a pass.

Crash: Running toward the hoop after a shot is taken to get a rebound, called "crashing the boards."

Cut: Another move without the ball. The player dashes into or across the lane looking for a pass.

Defense: The endeavor to get possession of the ball and prevent the opposition from scoring points.

Deny: The endeavor to prevent a player being open for a pass by blocking the passing lane with the body or at least an arm.

Double-team: Two on one defense, usually in the corners, also called a trap. It also occurs by fronting and backing a big man underneath.

Dribble: To advance the ball by bouncing it with either hand. The feet can do no more than a pivot move after a dribble. Once the dribble is stopped, it can't start again or a double-dribble violation is called. Dribbles can be behind the back or between the legs to keep the ball away from a defender.

Drive: A running dribble toward the hoop for a shot up close.

Dunk: A shot in which the player places the ball directly into the hoop, also called a slam, stuff, jam. If the player spins 180°, it's a reverse slam. Watch Michael Jordan, he's the best ever at this. (See Figure A.)

Fake: The art of getting a defender off balance or moving in one direction so you can move in another. The player usually moves the head or the ball, or even takes a step in one direction and then suddenly goes in another. A player can also fake a shot, called a pump fake, to get the defender to jump, and then the shooter goes up as the defender comes down. Players can put a series of fakes together to get a defender off balance.

Fast break: Moving the ball up court quickly by virtue of a long pass to a player streaking up court. The defense never gets set. The team fast breaking uses their speed and needs endurance.

Flash: Quick movements from one side of the free throw lane to the other, usually by a big player posting up at one side then flashing across the lane to the other.

Follow-up: Moving to the boards after taking a shot. Usually the player fades to the opposite side of the court from the shot since most rebounds bounce to the opposite side.

Forward: In the early days, these were offensive players who were allowed to move across the mid-court line and play offense. Now, the term refers to the tall players who take a position near the baseline on either side of the hoop. More and more these days, coaches just assign numbers to positions and areas.

Foul: Illegal contact between two players with any part of the body. The player causing the contact gets the foul, the other team gets possession or a shot depending on the type of foul. A personal foul is contact with an opponent. A common foul is a personal foul which is neither flagrant, intentional nor committed against a player trying for a field goal. An intentional foul is violent or savage. A technical foul is a non-contact foul. A player contact foul, also known as a charge, is committed by a ball handler.

Free throw: A free shot awarded to a player who is fouled. The shot is taken from the free throw line, 15 feet from the hoop.

Free throw lane: The 12-foot-wide area bounded by the free throw lines, also called the paint, inside the lane or underneath This area is where most of the action occurs in basketball.

Freeze: A type of offense which patiently, slowly controls the ball, either to waste time on the clock or to wait for a high percentage shot. Pete Carril coaches that way at Princeton University. The scores are always low, and it's boring. The pros don't allow it; I don't like it.

Front: Similar to "deny." The player blocks the passing lane with his body to deny a pass, usually to a big player. Unlike denying, which can occur anywhere, fronting always occurs underneath.

Game: Usually four six-minute quarters in grammar school and four eight-minute quarters in high school with a ten-minute halftime. If the game ends in a tie, three-minute overtime quarters are played until one ends with a team ahead in score. Teams get four time-outs per game and one additional for each overtime.

Give and go: The bread-and-butter play of basketball. A pass to a teammate, a dash toward the hoop past your defender, and a return pass for the lay-up. It's used far too infrequently.

Gooseneck: The position of the hand and forearm after a shot, resembling a goose's neck.

Guard: The name given to the players who bring the ball up court. They used to be defensive players only, guarding the defensive area, not allowed past mid-court. The point guard is the play-maker, a ball handler. The off guard is a shooting guard.

Inbounds: The playing area. A ball is passed from out-of-bounds after a field goal (a basket) or any time the ball goes out of bounds. A player has only five seconds to inbound and must start from the spot designated by the referee, except after a field goal.

Jab: A fake pivot step toward a defender to drive her back and get some room for a shot or pass. A reverse jab does the opposite, heading away from the basket and then breaking toward it. Also called a rocker step.

Jump ball: The opening play of the game. Two players meet at mid-court and the referee throws the ball up between them. They must tap it to teammates who are waiting outside the large mid-court circle. Jump shots used to occur whenever two opposing players were in equal possession of the ball, but now they just award it alternatively to either team (to speed up the game).

Jump shots: See Shots.

Jump stop: A key play not often taught to kids, yet it's an essential of footwork. Whenever a moving player comes to catch a pass or a rebound, he should jump onto both feet on the balls of the toes, so that either foot can then be a pivot. It also sets up the balanced triple-threat position.

Key: The term used to designate the area including the free throw lane and the free throw circle. The top of the key, the point of the circle farthest from the hoop, is the area where most plays are initiated.

Lay-up: See Shots.

Lob: A high pass over a defender, usually a fast break pass to a streaking guard or a pass over a defender fronting a player underneath.

Man-to-Man: One-on-one defense, guarding a specific player instead of an area.

Offense: The endeavor to score points by making field goals. A motion offense uses speed, screens and shooting ability; a power offense looks for the big players underneath.

Officials: They make sure the game is played by the rules. Basketball officials are the most harassed people in all sports. The game is fast and the fans are very close. This leads to much disagreement. The official referee signals of the National Federation of State High School Associations are reproduced in Figure G.

Outlet: A wing player, near the sideline, who sets up for a pass from a defensive rebounder. The idea is to set up away from any defenders so the rebounder can get the ball quickly out from underneath.

Overshift: Defending off center, to the strong side of a player. If a player is right-handed, we shift a bit to that side, placing the left foot forward blocking that lane.

Palm: The part of the hand that should touch the ball only rarely. Basketball is a finger game. In the early days, a palm ball was a violation if the hand made contact while dribbling with the underside of the ball.

Perimeter: The outside edge of the normal shooting distance—normally about 17 to 19 feet from the hoop. In college ball, a basket from the 19 foot, 9 inch distance scores three points. In the pros, it's from 21 feet. This is called the three-point line.

Period: A game is divided into four periods or quarters of 6 to 8 minutes each, depending on the level of play.

NATIONAL FEDERATION OFFICIAL BASKETBALL SIGNALS

NATIONAL FEDERATION
OFFICIAL BASKETBALL SIGNALS

1. Start clock
2. Stop clock or do not start clock — plus 19 toward the table for radio/TV time-out
3. Stop clock for jump ball
4. Beckon substitute ball dead - clock stopped
5. Stop clock for foul
6. Technical foul
7. Blocking
8. Holding
9. Pushing or charging
10. Illegal use of hand
11. Player control foul
12. A. Intentional foul B. Double foul
13. Traveling
14. Illegal dribble
15. 3 second violation *Open hand - run end line
16. Over and back or carrying the ball
17. Free throw, or designated spot violation
18. 5 or 10 second violation - use both hands for 10
19. Direction signal AND PLUS
20. Designates out-of-bounds spot
21. No score
22. OR Goal counts or is awarded
23. AND Point(s) scored (use 1 or 2 fingers)
19. PLUS Direction signal
24. Bonus free throw for 2nd throw drop 1 arm - for 2 throws use 1 arm with 2 fingers *Free throw violation by B
25. Lack of Action Prior to Warning After Warning Point Toward Team Responsible
26. 3-Point Field Goal Attempt And If Successful

Pick: Screening a defender who is guarding a player with the ball so he can dribble around the defender.

Pivot: Stepping and stretching in any direction with one foot, while the toes of the other foot are in continuous contact with the floor. The pivot foot can spin, but not lift or slide.

Point: The area at the top of the key from which most plays commence.

Post: See chapter one. The area underneath the basket. This term also describes a move by which a big player screens his defender with his back while awaiting a pass, and then rolls to either side to score.

Press: Full-court defense. This is an endeavor to harass and frustrate the players bringing the ball up court. The pressure will, you hope, force a mistake leading to a turnover.

Quarter: See Period.

Rebound: A missed shot which caroms off the rim or backboard onto the field of play. The attempt to secure this loose ball is called rebounding.

Scissor: A play whereby two offensive players crisscross in front of a third player, usually at a high post.

Screen: Gaining a set position in a lane and thereby preventing a defender from moving thus freeing the player defended. Used interchangeably with the term "pick," although screen often refers to a play off the ball.

Scrimmage: A practice game, usually intra-squad.

Shin splints: A common ailment involving pain in the shin area, sometimes quite painful. They often occur on harder surfaces or before a player is properly conditioned. Socks should always be worn at full height to keep this area warm.

Shots: There are many. The lay-up and jump shot are the dominant shots. Chippies are shots from directly underneath the net. Set shots are jump shots without a jump, usually from a far, undefended distance. A foul shot is a set shot. Underneath, we also have hook shots and dunks. Short jump shots often use the backboard in a bank shot. Three-point shots are from about 19 feet 9 inches or farther away. A fade away shot is just that, a fading backward jump shot. Some shots get their name from the floor position from which the shot is taken, e.g., corner, top of the key, half-court, high post. A double-pump is a fake shot followed by a shot off a lay-up. Names of shots also vary a bit by region. But the bread-and-butter are the lay-ups and jumpers, and that's where kids should start.

Shuffle: A motion or continuity pattern offensive play whereby all players continuously move according to a set pattern, looking for opportunities to score.

Soft-touch: A term used to identify short shots which softly hit the rim and drop in. They usually flow from good form, good ball control and hand coordination.

Square: Setting the shoulders perpendicular or slightly angled to the hoop before shooting. The main idea is one of balance and being set.

Stall: Boring! This is an attempt to waste time by passing around the perimeter. Some teams use it to slow down the tempo or keep the score close against a better team. It used to be allowed forever so the shot clock was instituted to require a team to shoot in 24 seconds in the pros or 45 seconds in college games. There is no shot clock in youth basketball. Stalling is just not basketball!

Strong side: Often, especially against a zone defense, teams will place an extra man to one side. This also happens naturally on the side the ball is on.

Superman: A drill for shooting or rebounding consecutively and alternately from each side of the basket, back and forth.

Switch: A defensive move when two offensive players crisscross or pick and roll; they switch and guard each other's man.

Ten seconds: The amount of time given to inbound and bring the ball past mid-court after a change of possession.

Tip: To tap the ball to another player or toward the hoop without catching it. Used often to steal passes or tap rebounds.

Trailer: A player who follows a driving ball handler to the hoop. He will often shout "trailer" to alert the player that he is ready for a dump pass backward or a rebound.

Transition: The change from offense to defense or vice versa. Quickness and alertness here can make a difference.

Trap: Double-teaming a player with the ball, usually in a corner or along the sideline.

Travel: To take two steps without dribbling.

Triple-threat: The balanced offensive or defensive stance from which a player can move in any direction with equal ease.

Turnover: Losing possession to the other team while dribbling or because of a bad pass.

Underneath: Home to the big players under the hoop. The heartland of basketball.

Walking: Taking two steps without a dribble.

Zone: The poor man's defense. The zone defense is not as skillful as the man-to-man, trying more to clog up the area closest to the basket, thus forcing outside shots.

INDEX